Today, you stand at a c... branch out in every direction. Some are narrow, ... and wind away into dense woods only a few yards from where you stand. Others are wide, smooth, and run slightly downhill to what seem to be pleasant valleys.

But which lead to a life that is wise, good, and free, and which will take you to hell on earth (and maybe beyond)? You certainly can't tell from where you stand. And you can't stay here, you have to keep moving. What should you do? How should you choose?

Do not necessarily take the path with the most footsteps on it—although that is no reason to reject it. There may be a very good reason it is the path less chosen. And do not just "follow your heart" or whatever bad advice you've picked up from movies or song lyrics.

You will have to trust and use your map, even when it seems to lead you in directions you might not have guessed or chosen. Your map is the accumulated experience of those who have come this way before you. It is the lessons they learned—and paid for—in blood. It is told in their stories, and written in their books. It is the wealth of the generations. This book is part of that map.

Be wise, do good, and live free.

Be Wise, Do Good, Live Free

Random Advice for the Best Kind of Life

Gregory Smith

Copyright © 2012 by Gregory Smith

This is a work of nonfiction. Any resemblance to actual persons, organizations or events are purely coincidence.

All rights reserved by the author, including the right of reproduction in whole or in part in any form.

Cover design by Greg Smith of Black Lake Studio.

Published by Black Lake Press of Holland, Michigan.
Black Lake Press is a division of Black Lake Studio, LLC.
Direct inquiries to Black Lake Press at www.blacklakepress.com.

ISBN 978-0-9839602-5-6

Dedication

To Andrew and Maggie, and to all "my" students at Manna Vintage Faith and Downtown Student Fellowship. Please grow up to be better than me and my generation. Be wiser, better, and live more freely than we have.

Table of Contents

Acknowledgements	9
Introduction	11
Random Advice for the Wise, Good, and Free Life	15
Ten Things That I Wish Someone Had Told Me When…	157
• I Was a Teenager	159
• I Got Married	167
• I Started a Business	175
Ten Success Myths that Are Ruining Your Performance and Killing Your Career	185
Five Ways to Fail in Business, and Six to Succeed	191
About the Author	199

Acknowledgements

This book is my meager attempt to distill the advice (or at least as I have understood it) of generations of men and women who have already walked this way—the Wealth of the Generations. I thank them, and their writings over the centuries. I don't know where to begin listing all the books that have shaped my understanding of the world, but I cannot imagine my life without the wisdom of their words.

More than anyone else, my wife Linda is responsible for this book because she has made it possible for me to write it. Being a writer's spouse is not an easy job, but for twenty-six years she has graciously helped me to become the person I am. I could not have written it without her love, encouragement, assistance, common sense, patience, and—yes, I'll say it—endurance.

Every day I strive (usually without success) to be worthy of my children. I'm proud of my son Andrew, a wise, good, and free young man who inspires me to be a better old(er) man. My daughter Maggie is everything a dad could want in a daughter, and will always be my princess.

My parents, J.D. and Sandra, gave me a realistic view of the world and human nature. They taught me to love books, language, and learning. They gave me a fierce love of individual liberty and respect for the heritage of America. My in-laws, Rod and Laura Mulder, have supported us in many ways over the years, and are models of the wise, good, and free life.

Rob Stam is a rock in my world (not a stone in my shoe). He constantly encourages me to write books, and his hard work at Black Lake Studio & Press allows me to do it. Mike Dokter at Black Lake supports my delusions of grandeur, tells the world about the tacos, and clicks the PowerPoint like nobody's business.

My editorial interns at Black Lake are incredible, no less for their patience with the chaos I create than for their heroic efforts to turn my comma-strewn and grammatically-challenged rants into legible and literate prose. Sam Tzou continues to be brilliant and gracious, with a servant's heart, who I expect to make the world measurably better. Jessica Simmons (soon to be Sjoholm) intimidates me with her intelligence, amazes me with her eye for detail, and inspires me with her willingness to help. Michael Brooks is a wordsmith-in-waiting, who will soon be writing books that he might let me proofread, although I'm not sure he will need it. All of them did great work scrubbing this manuscript, and anything that's not clean and well-said is my fault.

My deep thanks and affection to everyone at Manna Vintage Faith, for giving us a home and me a place to think out loud. Thanks to the students who sat through my study of the Book of Proverbs: this book began with those brown-bag lunches.

Barbara Yandell continues to encourage and entertain Linda and I. Her prayers and practical wisdom are scattered throughout these pages (even though she is unlikely to read them due to her limited, uh, *schedule...*). I'm looking forward to us all living wise, good, and free on the compound, someday.

Introduction

How to Read This Book

Feel free to skip this introduction and start reading anywhere in this book. The title is accurate: the advice in this book is organized randomly (if that isn't an oxymoron). My goal is to offer insight as life demands it, for we encounter this world's joys and challenges with little apparent pattern. And so, I figured, any attempt to prioritize or categorize these bits of advice would probably throw some readers off: if they started in a chapter about money when they were really struggling with relationships, the book wouldn't seem relevant, or vice versa. So I've mostly laid them out by how they fit on the page or in the order I edited them in, and I hope that the reader will flip through the pages and stumble upon something that is relevant to his or her day.

Go back and forth, close your eyes and stick your finger somewhere inside. Read odd-numbered proverbs on odd-numbered days and even on even. Find something that works.

Near the back of the book I broke down and organized some lists: ten things that I wish someone had told me when I was a teenager, etc. But within those lists, there is no thematic structure. I just wrote them down in the order they occurred to me.

What this Book is About

In my life and travels, I have observed two kinds of people. They are not divided by race, class, gender, politics, religion, education, or wealth.

The first group is made up of people who are shrewd and decent. They avoid bad decisions, habits, and relationships that limit their liberty. They are not necessarily the richest, the winners of every contest, or the most popular. While they face the same external crises and challenges as everyone else, these people not only survive; they bounce back better than ever and move on. While they make mistakes, they only make them once and sometimes not even that. They don't just learn the hard way; they take advice and often manage to avoid most of the pitfalls in the first place. They don't make too many unforced errors. They are ethical and make the world a better place because of their presence in it. In short, they are wise, they do good, and they live free.

The second group's lives are characterized by foolish decisions, vices, poor performance, and enslavement—to debts, bad relationships and habits, addictions, mediocrity, and the consequences of their poor choices. They roll down the highway of life, barely in control, swerving from side to side, banging into the guard rails until they are dented and wobbling, unable to hold a straight line any longer.

In short, the first group can handle what life throws at them, and the second cannot.

If you would place yourself in the second group up to this point, I have some good news: you are not a victim or doomed to live this way forever. Wisdom, goodness and freedom can be learned. If you value it, seek it, and train yourself in it, you can be wise, do good, and live free.

This book is a meager attempt (like the biblical *Book of Proverbs,* or *Poor Richard's Almanac,* or George Washington's *Rules of Civility*) to compile some of the Wisdom of the Generations—the tried and true lessons that our forefathers paid for in blood so that we wouldn't have to repeat their mistakes—and to apply them to life in the United States of America at the beginning of the 21st century.

The secrets to living wise, good, and free are not really secrets at all. They are common sense, but not always common behaviors. Listen to them and and then *do* them, lest you look back on a life that was foolish, evil, and enslaved.

One more thing, and then you can pick a page and start reading. Wisdom, goodness, and freedom are ends, not means. We don't attempt them so that we can become rich or famous, make a mark in history, or earn a slot in heaven. Strive to live wise, good, and free because that's what you were made to become, a reflection of God's image. It is the best way to live.

— Greg Smith

Random Advice for the Wise, Good, and Free Life

- 1 -

The tree of liberty must be refreshed from time to time with the clean water of self-reliance.

Thomas Jefferson famously said that, "The tree of liberty must be refreshed from time to time with the blood of patriots and tyrants." He wrote that after an uprising during the early years of the United States, Shay's Rebellion. Taxes were raised to pay for high government debt and chaos in the currency markets. Sound familiar? Jefferson was arguing that the government had to be accountable—and in a genuinely free nation always would be—to the citizens. If the government exceeded its mandate, it had to expect a reaction from the people.

But an overreaching government is not the only, or even the most common, restriction on our liberty. Every day, we trade our freedom away for security.

There is nothing wrong with getting a helping hand, and even less with giving one. But every unearned dollar we take makes us a little less free. Even though the giver may be graceful and expect nothing in return, the more we rely on the generosity of others, the less we can make our own decisions and the less we own our accomplishments. One of the great moments in life is to point to something that we built, or something that we earned with our brains, brawn, and effort, and say, "I did that!" I feel sad when I see those who will never be able to own their success, because they were afraid or unable to risk failure. When you can't fail, you can't really succeed.

As Jefferson said, a free people must hold their government accountable. But before they can do that, they must hold themselves accountable. The idea that became America, despite all its many flaws of execution, is that we should rely first on ourselves to make our own success. That makes us free men and women, and it gives us a right to be led by a government that preserves our liberties.

There is nothing wrong with depending on others, or accepting some help when you really need it. But every dollar you get from someone else makes you a little bit less free. The tree of liberty is nourished by the water of self-reliance.

• • •

- 2 -

We have lost the idea of honor, and we are a worse people without it.

The concept of honor was a fixture of civilization for thousands of years. Of course, it was an ideal like chastity or charity that we didn't always live up to, but at least we aspired to it. We measured ourselves by it, and held others accountable to it. To label a man or woman honorable or dishonorable was to say something important about them.

Honor wasn't hereditary. You could be born noble, but you could not inherit honor. You couldn't buy or borrow it. You weren't entitled to it; there was no right to honor. It couldn't be demanded or given, only earned. As Liam Neeson's character in the 1995 movie *Rob Roy* tells his children, "Honor is the gift a man gives himself."

Honor is like a bank account of your wisdom, goodness, and freedom. A fool cannot be honorable. A bad man or woman is not honorable. You are not honorable if you squander your liberty with drink, debt, or a thousand other masters that can enslave a life.

Honor is expensive, but it doesn't cost money. Honor is accrued through a shrewd mind, integrity, courage, honesty, decency, virtue, self-discipline, and a fierce commitment to take as much responsibility as possible for your own life.

Yes, the idea of honor was sometimes abused. Some people who claimed it didn't deserve it, but that didn't invalidate the ideal. And yes, honor can lead to the spiritual disease of pride, but it doesn't have to. Properly understood, it is self-correcting: an arrogant man is dishonorable.

For all its potential faults, a society with the ideal of honor is better than one without it, in which we are defined as a helpless bag of offended victimhood and entitled rights that demand to be filled, regardless of our merit.

America's Founding Fathers enumerated some rights in the Declaration of Independence: the right to life, liberty, and the pursuit of happiness (not happiness, but its pursuit, which is a crucial distinction). We are entitled to an opportunity to earn honor. We have a right to choose wisdom, goodness, and freedom. But over the years, we have so diluted the notion of personal responsibility that honor no longer has a place in our social contract. We now assert that just because someone is foolish, immoral, or voluntarily enslaves themselves to debt, destructive behavior, or bad relationships, they should not be disqualified from their right to everything from housing and healthcare, cell phones and all the erectile dysfunction drugs they "need."

But if nothing can be our fault, then nothing can be to our credit. If it is impossible to be dishonorable, then no one can earn honor. Forget winning in modern America: all the players get a participant's ribbon. As a nation, we have defined ourselves by the lowest common denominator, and then we wonder where all the honorable men and women went.

Yes, our Founding Fathers enshrined the rights to life, liberty, and the pursuit of happiness in the Declaration of Independence. But do you know how they signed it? This is the last sentence of that document:

And for the support of this Declaration, with a firm reliance on the protection of Divine Providence, we mutually pledge to each other our Lives, our Fortunes, and our sacred Honor.

No one in our public life talks like that anymore, and we are not better off because of it.

Thomas Jefferson, the primary author of the Declaration, once said, "Nobody can acquire honor by doing what is wrong." Ironically, Jefferson was a tragic figure. We all know about his brilliance and accomplishments: few have written more eloquently about wisdom, goodness, and freedom. But his life was marked by foolishness, bad behavior, and denial of liberty—his own enslavement to debt and his personal enslavement of men, women, and children (he acknowledged slavery was wrong, but he could never bring himself to free his own slaves, even in his will). Jefferson understood honor, but I don't think he was an honorable man.

Anyone who delights in mocking the ideals Jefferson could not live up to and erecting in their place a culture of shrill and slouching mediocrity should remember the words of two other presidents. In his Gettysburg Address, Abraham Lincoln said that only time would tell if a government of the people, by the people, for the people would perish from the earth. The United States was intended to be a reflection of the American people. If we are dishonorable, our country will be too. And in 1916, Woodrow Wilson said, "The nation's honor is dearer than the nation's comfort; yes, than the nation's life itself."

The world needs America to be a wise, good, and free nation. That begins with me, and you. Our lives, our fortunes, and our sacred honor are at stake.

• • •

- 3 -

Don't fall for the singer who makes millions traveling the world singing songs about how miserable they are traveling the world as a millionaire singing songs. One, or both of you, are idiots.

• • •

- 4 -

A society can argue about what is moral, but when it argues whether there is even such a thing as morality, it is in trouble. When it ridicules people for having any morals at all, it is doomed.

Large swaths of our society are committing mass cultural suicide. Exhausted by ethical arguments and driven by religious convictions, many of us have thrown up our hands, concluding that since we can't agree on what is moral, nothing must be. Many of us have decided that morality is a matter of personal preference, that there are no transcendent rules that bind us, other than to leave each other alone to follow our own bliss.

A civilization is a tenuous thing. It's held together by not only shared values, but by mutual trust that those values are shared and that they will be honored and upheld. When that trust is shattered, we form protective bonds with those we can trust to hold sacred the things we love. When we reach that point, we descend into tribes and build feudal castles we can fall back into when our lands are being ravaged. A society that believes that good and evil are matters of personal taste is headed for "interesting times."

But when we mock the concept of good and evil, when those who live by a moral code are ridiculed for believing in something bigger themselves and their own pleasures, then revolution is just over the horizon. For the evidence offended history is that such a society cannot long endure. Big ideas drive the world, and those who refuse to believe in them never see what is coming.

• • •

- 5 -

You are smack-dab in the middle of the only life you will ever get.

We like to daydream about the other lives we might lead, or might have led. We think about other choices we could have made or about what lies over the vast horizon five or ten years from now. We are seduced by our potential and imagine that someday we might be better people, in better places, doing better things.

And so we might. But the clock is ticking, and the testimony of every senior citizen I've ever met is that time seems to accelerate as you age. One day you wake up and you're old. You never noticed it slipping by.

Yes, so much is possible. But if you don't move quickly, it becomes less probable every day. There are no do-overs or re-takes, and no one gets a reset button. This is not a rehearsal, this is your life, the only one you will ever get. Stop fantasizing and lying to yourself about what you will do tomorrow or next year. Do it now.

• • •

- 6 -

Courage is not fearlessness. Fools are fearless. Courage is doing the right thing, even when you are terrified.

I don't trust people who are never afraid, and I don't want to do anything dangerous with them. I grew up climbing and sailing, and I was taught at an early age to be afraid of the ocean and the mountains. They are pretty, but they are not your friends. They don't care about you: that pretty blue wave will drown you without an apology, and a moment's carelessness on that beautiful ridge will leave you freezing or falling to your death. I don't want to be roped to the fool who doesn't take this climb seriously. And in business, just like sports and war, people do get hurt. Don't enter the arena casually.

On the other hand, I don't trust people who cannot master their fears. Courage is not being carefree; it is being in control of oneself. Our animal instincts scream at us to fight or flee, but the wise, good, and free person chooses. He or she doesn't just react. They think and judge and decide. Courage is when your head and heart rule your limbs, when your values hold your imagination in check. A courageous person contains their fear and uses it to take calculated risks. Courage slows your pulse, calms your breathing, measures your words, guides your decisions and rests your mind on the right course of action. Courage doesn't second guess or look back.

The bold man doesn't think. The brave man thinks, and chooses to be bold when it's the right thing to do. That is the way of wisdom, goodness, and freedom.

• • •

- 7 -

How to become a writer: stop telling me what you're going to write and show me what you've written.

I meet too many folks whose ambitions are just lifestyle aspirations. Actually, they are daydreams of a lifestyle, which they imagine come with a certain career. Kids aspire to be rockstars or pro athletes, but they don't daydream about the hard work or the practice, they imagine parties and private planes. Middle aged men dream about being their own boss, with time and money and prestige to spare, not the toil of running a business.

These daydreams are so seductive that many stall out in their efforts to make their ambitions actual. Here's the subtle trap: because we are attracted to the lifestyle, we begin to adopt some of the trappings of that lifestyle because it feels like we are getting closer to our dreams. We pick the low hanging fruit and gorge on it, ignoring the harder work of climbing the tree, or planting our own tree.

For example, I meet lots of people who want to be writers. Why do they want to be writers? Do they enjoy writing? Maybe a little bit: they dabble in blogging or write an occasional newsletter piece. Some have a novel they've been working on for six years, a couple of short stories they've started, or a great idea for a nonfiction book. But turning those into finished products and selling them for money is hard work. Deep down inside, their dream is not to write, but to "be a writer." So instead, they begin to adopt the trappings of what they imagine is a writer's life: they hang out in coffee shops, or attend literary conferences, or wander through bookstores.

Do you want to be a professional writer? Then write. A lot. Learn how to write what will sell, and do that. The same is true for any other endeavor; there is no shortcut to doing the work.

• • •

- 8 -

Conservatives are at an inherent disadvantage in elections. What are they supposed to say? "Vote for us, we'll do less?" But sometimes, the best cure for current problems *is* for the government to do less.

• • •

- 9 -

That thing that someone did to you that you've been carrying around for years? That makes you angry and hurt and keeps you stuck where you are, in a small world? Yeah, that one. Listen, it's not worth it. Let. It. Go.

Someone wronged you somehow, sometime. OK. So what?

First of all, there are over six billion people alive today. Paleodemographers (who study ancient population sizes and mortality rates) estimate that the total number of people who have ever lived is between 100 and 115 billion. Even if the actual number were only half of that, that's still fifty billion souls. Question: how many of those fifty billion had someone mistreat them sometime, somehow? How many of those lives were marred by injustice, cruelty, neglect, or unrequited love? How many were disrespected or not taken seriously by a family member or neighbor? How many had opportunities denied, or didn't get what they felt they deserved? Most? Yes, whatever it was that someone did to you wasn't fair, right, or considerate. But that's not unique or special.

So now what? It's been eating away your insides for years. It's been corrosive to your soul, your sleep, and your social life. You don't grow; you just churn the same hurt and bile and envy and resentment over and over. It's your right to do so, of course. But the clock is running on your life. This isn't making you wiser, better, or more free. In fact, it is holding you in bondage and making you a smaller person.

How much of your life do you want this to steal from you? Let it go. Do something constructive with your time and opportunities. Grow a large enough soul that the poison from your pain is diluted in a sea of wisdom, goodness, and freedom.

• • •

- 10 -

Names and dates are not all that is important about history, but they are important. They are the minimum that you need to know. Never let yourself be lectured about how the world got the way it is by people who can't at least get the facts straight.

Of course history is more than a series of names and dates. Who ever said it was? Even the ancient historians, as far back as Herodotus in the fifth century B.C., wrote about how? and why?, not just who? and when?

But if you don't know the who and when, then all the how and why stuff becomes a jumbled up mess of speculation and confused narrative. Before you know it, you're babbling on about how the hopes of the Inca people were crushed by the values of the British Empire through the bayonets of the redcoats and unfair tea pricing, or how Leonardo DaVinci stole his design for the first washing machine from the Ashanti Kingdom of West Africa.

This is especially galling in the age of smart phones, with the compendium of human knowledge in our palms while we speak. If you are so smart, how come you can't get the continents and centuries straight? Take a moment, and at least check Wikipedia.

It's one thing to say that the world is complex and that we need to follow the backstories and peel back the layers to catch its nuances. But do not let anyone use that as an excuse for being too lazy or unconcerned with reality to learn the basic facts. Be careful when they bloviate: that fog might carry an agenda. "Don't worry about the facts," they will say. "Pay attention to my *larger point*..." The wise, good, and free person knows to watch out, because someone is trying to sell him something.

• • •

- 11 -

Sex is like fire: used for the right purpose, it warms you, brings joy, and is useful in the home. Misused, it can devour you, burn down your house, and kill your family. Don't be an arsonist or careless with sparks. Enjoy hearth and home.

• • •

- 12 -

Yoda said, "Spiritual beings we are, not this crude matter." He was wrong. We are matter, and it's not crude. God breathed life into it.

Don't despise your body. You can be unhappy with how it looks or performs, or frustrated with its diseases or decay. But don't see having it as a liability or a limitation. It's a privilege and a blessing.

There were religions and movements in the ancient world based on the notion that our bodies, and the entire material realm, are made of an inferior stuff when compared with the pure forms of energy and spirit. According to this view, we are ghosts trapped in this crude machine, until we can escape back into the ethereal realm. Even some Christians talk this way, imagining how much better it would be to fly like the angels instead of being stuck in traffic.

But we are material beings and have never been anything but. The Book of Genesis tells us that God scooped up some of the dirt of the earth and breathed life into it. It's important to note that it wasn't the other way around: we weren't the spirits who were given bodies, but clumps of matter that were given souls.

We have the joy of being part of this universe, not being trapped within it. We can smell a rose and have our finger pricked by its thorn. We can laugh until our drinks come out our noses, feel tired from a day's work, and taste our food. We can see the sun through our eyelids and feel its warmth on our cheeks. We can get drunk from wine, wake up with coffee, and get ice cream headaches. We can smell the salt of the ocean before we can see the beach. And everything about sex is funny and weird and yet very OK, but what would be the point without bodies?

To be human is to know the joys and sorrows of our bodies and to run the risks while racing against the clock of our mortality. There is no alternative, even if you wished for one. God likes the material world: he invented it. The wise, good, and free person doesn't despise his body; he treats it well and uses it as best he can.

• • •

- 13 -

The "Good Old Days" were always thirty or forty years ago, because that's when the person describing them was young, the world seemed new, and they had their whole life ahead of them.

• • •

- 14 -

The correct word to describe someone who lacks the goodness to use their freedom wisely is a "tragedy."

It has been pointed out that, "Youth is wasted on the young." The older you get, the more you think about the things you would have done differently if only you knew then what you know now. All the opportunity and energy and potential that come with being young are usually not accompanied by the wisdom to use it properly. Young people fritter away what old people long to have another shot at. That's why young people should listen to their elders and the wealth of the generations. But they never have and probably never will. That's one of the paradoxes of our mortality: maturity waxes while muscle wanes.

But there is another kind of wasted opportunity that we cannot blame on the cycle of life. Far too often, we squander liberty. Freedom may not be rare, but it is precious. It can be invested like an annuity, enjoyed like a great meal, gifted through love to bless another, or spent on a worthy cause. It takes wisdom to not waste our freedom, and goodness and discipline to set goals for how to spend it.

But how often have you wasted free time? You could have done something constructive or compassionate, or just had fun. Instead, you did nothing. That freedom slipped through your fingers.

The Internet offers freedom that a thousand generations could only dream of: freedom to learn, to share, to create, to enjoy, to invest in a better future. Instead, we aimlessly surf social media and shopping sites and watch pointless video clips. Given a liberty of time, space, and knowledge that Thomas Jefferson could not have imagined, after three hours online we have nothing to show for it.

We waste our freedom to travel and we waste the freedom that the money in our pocket gives us. We waste our freedom of speech, religion, and assembly. We waste the opportunities our relationships give us.

Are we decent and disciplined enough to use our freedom wisely? It's a tragedy if we are not.

• • •

- 15 -

Walk a lot. Enjoy the world from ground level, at a human scale and pace.

Don't be a Luddite (19th century textile workers who destroyed the looms of the industrial revolution to protest change and force society to return to a pre-industrial world). It's a good thing that we can fly like birds, commute to work at five times the speed of a horse, and that moving to a distant city doesn't mean we will never see our family again. Only a fool—a dishonest fool, because he almost certainly enjoys not traveling in the hold of a ship—would deny that.

But when we fly like birds and sit in boxes of steel and glass that slide us toward our destination while we surf the Web, we become disconnected from the joyful limits of our own bodies. I love looking out the window of an airplane at the shape of a coast, or the twists and turns of the Grand Canyon, or the hodgepodge of Britain's hedgerows. But while that perspective is a spectacular gift—the viewpoint of the ancient gods—really knowing those places requires seeing them from a human scale. It means smelling the salt blowing across the beach, or watching the shadows recede from the canyon walls overhead as the sun briefly passes over at noon, or dodging cow dung as you inhale the scent of the fresh grass and search for the gate in a dry stone wall.

It is not a curse to be human, to see the world from five or six feet off of the ground, to move at three or four miles per hour, and to rest tired feet at the end of the day.

A wise, good, and free man is self-reliant, and one physical manifestation of self-reliance is the simple act of moving your body around under its own power (as much as you can, depending on your physical ability).

So embody wisdom, goodness, and freedom: carry your own stuff, on your own two feet, at your own pace, as much as you can.

• • •

- 16 -

If guys planned weddings, you could get married next Saturday.

• • •

- 17 -

Don't value wisdom, or goodness, or freedom over (or to the exclusion of) the others on that list. That is a distorted vision of mankind. History has taught us that all of them must work together.

Other cultures have valued one of these virtues over the other, or to the exclusion of the others. But a wise man who is neither good nor free is merely a sage, a shrewd operator, or a manipulator.

A good man who is neither wise nor free is an innocent who will often stumble through life as a victim of people or circumstances.

A free man who is neither wise nor good is a libertine, who will eventually squander his freedom with foolish and bad choices and will leave nothing of value behind.

The exceptional vision of Western culture that became the idea of America (however we have struggled to live up to our ideals), is of wise and good men who know how to use their liberty to make the world a better place than they found it.

I have two fears. First, I worry that America is being torn by competing subcultures that value one of these virtues and denigrate the other two. We put forth various distorted visions for our individual and collective lives instead of a common ideal of people who use their liberty to become as wise as snakes and as innocent as doves.

My other fear is that we are becoming a culture that values none of them. When our leaders and heroes are fools and bad people, enslaved to their passions, to debt, etc., then we are on the road to ruin. Historically, that sometimes has led to restoration of a nation, but only after revolutionary change. It would be best if we could avoid that cycle.

• • •

- 18 -

Some fears are magical: the more we think about them, the more they become prophecies.

A healthy dose of fear can keep you alive. If you can imagine worst-case scenarios, you can prepare for them, and fortune favors the prepared mind.

But here is weird phenomenon: sometimes, worst-case scenarios become self-fulfilling prophecies. Sometimes, we imagine what might go wrong so powerfully that our obsession brings it to life.

For example, suppose you worry that you might lose your marriage, or your job. That might spur you to prevent it, or it might poison your interactions so that you become a defensive, tentative employee. Your paranoia might drive you to become a smothering or withdrawn spouse.

Fear can create the very reality that terrifies you. Your fear of failure might keep you from investing in things, or to try so hard to succeed that you drive people away. Your fears might keep you from taking necessary risks, corrupt your mind, or cause you to lash out when restraint is called for.

The secret of success is not to be fearless, for only fools are fearless. No, the trick is to master our fears, and to use them constructively. And there are three keys to mastering fear:

- **Self-Control.** Learn to control and focus your thoughts. Discipline your mind and imagination. Guard your speech, because talking too much about your fears breathes life into them. And speaking of breathing, pay attention to the mind-body connection by learning to control your breathing, pulse, and rest. A tired, hungry, stressed body is more prone to fear.
- **Faith.** Do you believe in God? I do, and my faith gives me a comfort and peace that is bigger than my fear. Undoubtedly, bad things will happen to me, but I know that this life is only part of my story. I am afraid of some things, but not very afraid.
- **Friends.** Courageous people inspire me, and their courage rubs off on me. Excessive fear and the cowardice it invokes are a disease, and I don't want to catch it. Love fear-ridden people, help them when you can and should, but don't let them infect you. Surround yourself with wise, good, and free people, and let their attitudes be your default state.

• • •

- 19 -

The wise sometimes choose to quit or retreat so that they can remain good and free. But they never just give up.

There is a difference between persistence and perseverance.

Persistent is a neutral, descriptive term. It means that you tend to continue to do whatever you are doing. You might persist in doing good, or in going the wrong direction. To persist in doing the wrong thing is no virtue. The wise, good, and free person knows when to quit. Not because something is hard, but because it's foolish, or bad, or squanders their freedom. Jesus said that if your hand or eye is doing evil, cut it off or pluck it out, because it's better to go to heaven maimed than to hell intact.

In fact, the wise person quits more quickly than the fool if he is on the wrong path. Why take another step away from goodness and freedom? Or the wise person may decide to slow down, or to retreat back to regroup and try again from another direction or with more resources.

But the wise, good, and free person never just gives up. They never quit something that is worthy just because it is hard or because their commitment wanes. They never quit out of disloyalty or fear. They never lose a fight because they lost faith or let down their friends.

That's the difference between persistence and perseverance. Persistence is a neutral quality, but to persevere is a virtue. It means to endure difficulty, to have strength in hard circumstances, to stand when it would be so easy to run. To persevere isn't to mindlessly continue in the wrong direction, but to see good things through to the end. It takes wisdom to choose a cause, but it takes goodness to persevere and preserve liberty.

• • •

- 20 -

Sometimes, you are so far into a mess, so far past the point of no return, that the shortest way out is to press on. Stop looking back. Don't whine. Work out the problem, and keep going until you're out the other side.

In Advice #19, I pointed out that the wise man knows when to quit, and that persistence isn't necessarily a virtue.

Sometimes, you have to quit forward. I remember talking to some of the rock climbers who scale the vast granite walls of Yosemite Valley. Some routes climb more than half a mile over the valley floor, and are overhung past vertical. This means that once climbers are at least a couple of rope lengths above the starting point, they cannot rappel back down, since the rope would hang too far out from the wall. The climbers explained that if one of them were to get sick or injured beyond this point of no return, the only way to get home is to continue climbing up to the valley rim where they can hike back to town. Since some of these routes can take a week to complete, any problems past the first day means six more days of climbing with a sick or injured partner. They called it "bailing up" instead of bailing out.

Sometimes, the only way out of a crisis is through it. American soldiers in World War II were in the service for the duration of the conflict or until they were dead or too injured to serve anymore. Winston Churchill, prime minister of Great Britain during that war, actually inspired the nation by bracing it for the reality that the only path to victory was to persevere through whatever lay ahead.

There is a dangerous softness growing in the center of our culture. It is not just weak thinking or sloppy morality. We have lost the virtue of fortitude: perseverance, grit, rawhide toughness. It is not necessarily a Christian virtue. It helped the three hundred Spartans at Thermopylae to hold their ground, it got Alexander's Macedonians to India and back, it kept Caesar's Tenth Legion in their ranks in the face of barbarian charges, it drove the Norsemen in their dragon ships across the cold waves to Newfoundland, and it was at the heart of the Samurai's code. Those pagan cultures had plenty of vices, but courage and fortitude were among their virtues.

Europeans today use "cowboy" as a derisive term for a certain American ideal, without seeming to understand that many of us admire the image of the cowboys, mountain men, and settlers who were tanned as leather and tough as nails. They gave us our liberty.

The problem with America today is that we don't have *enough* of the cowboy virtues. Wisdom, goodness, and freedom are earned and kept by tough and brave men and women who know how to hold ground, endure hardship, and press on to the finish—without whining or needing a support group. We are badly in need of more people like that. They are still among us, and we should be holding them up as our heroes and role models. We should, *must,* become a strong people once again. Then the truly weak, not merely the weak hearted, will be safe in the land of the free and the home of the brave.

• • •

- 21 -

If a person will lie to and cheat the spouse that they vowed before God to honor until death, or abandon the children who depend on them, why should I believe that they will be honest with me?

We all lie and cheat.

We've all told "little white lies:" took ten pounds off our weight for our driver's license or exaggerated our accomplishments in a job interview. We've counted words that weren't in the dictionary in Scrabble games or left a snack or two off our calorie counters. If we are really honest, then we have to admit that we haven't been really honest.

But while all deception is logically equal, some lies are more serious than others. Who we lie to, what we lie about, why we lie to them, and how that impacts them—these things do matter.

An oath to testify in court, or to defend your country as a soldier, or to uphold the Constitution in public office, is a sacred vow. That's why breaking those oaths leads to jail for perjury, dereliction of duty, or impeachment. If you lie and cheat at a

United States military academy, you invite dishonor and expulsion.

And when you bound yourself before God and a church full of witnesses to be faithful to a spouse, you accepted that the consequences of breaking that oath would be a loss of honor and trust. And yet some lie and cheat on their spouse and violate the trust of their family as easily as if they were telling a bill collector that they put the check in the mail yesterday.

I have friends who are convinced that "accountability groups" will keep people from making "poor choices" (falling into sin). I love the idea, but if someone will lie to their spouse and children, what keeps them from lying to their accountability group?

I'm not saying that people can't change after they violate their family's trust, but I certainly don't assume that they have. People have to earn trust. And the threshold to earn my trust is a bit higher for a proven adulterer.

• • •

- 22 -

Everyone knows there are seasons in life. Only the wise can forecast their changing.

We all know that timing matters. It's in the Bible, in the third chapter of the Book of Ecclesiastes:

> *There is a time for everything, and a season for every activity under the heavens:*
>
> > *a time to be born and a time to die,*
> >
> > *a time to plant and a time to uproot,*

a time to kill and a time to heal,
a time to tear down and a time to build,
…a time to search and a time to give up,
a time to keep and a time to throw away,
…a time to be silent and a time to speak,
a time to love and a time to hate,
a time for war and a time for peace.

It's not a special insight to point out that the seasons of life call for different courses of action. It's like saying that since the stock market goes up and down, we should buy low and sell high.

No, the trick in the market is to recognize when the market is going to change a few days (or minutes or seconds) before everyone else, and to make your moves before they do.

The great hockey player Wayne Gretzky was once asked how he scored so many goals in his career. He said that the other players skated to where the puck was, but he figured out where the puck was going to be and got there first.

To be wise, good, and free, we need to learn to read the changing of the seasons so that we can act appropriately. We must be shrewd enough to know what is right at the right time. Sometimes liberty is to be enjoyed, sometimes it is to be advanced, and sometimes it must be defended.

• • •

- 23 -

God can bless a faithful person, regardless of their effort. And self-reliance can crowd out faith. But still, if I have to bet on who will succeed in life, it's on the shrewd, industrious, and decent.

I believe to my marrow that faith can beat strength, skill, and self-reliance. David took down Goliath because he trusted God, and God guided the stone from his sling. The Bible, history, and my own personal experience convince me that God will bless those who bless him, and will bring down those who despise him.

God always blesses those who love and trust him in faith. They always succeed in God's endeavors. But they don't always succeed in their endeavors. I know people of great faith and devotion whose careers go nowhere, who can't build an organization or business to save their life, and who end up getting the short end of almost every deal they negotiate.

I can't help remembering the old joke: "The race is not always won by the swift, nor the battle by the strong. But that's the way to bet."

Faith, hope, and charity are the cardinal virtues of Christian faith. But there are foundational virtues like prudence (self-control and self-discipline), temperance (moderation in action, thought, and feeling), fortitude (courage and strength of mind to cope with danger or pain), and justice (doing the right thing).

God might answer the prayers of and grant success to someone who has not cultivated wisdom, is not decent and industrious, and who is mired in addictions, debt, and bad relationships. But the surest path to success is to become a faithful person who learns to be as wise as a serpent, is innocent as a dove, and treasures their liberty.

• • •

- 24 -

Foolishness, evil, and enslavement are more entertaining than happiness. No one wants to buy a song or watch a movie about happy, well-adjusted people who do their work, spend wisely, and love their families. Which is why, if you learn about the world from songs and movies, you will have a skewed and warped view of the world.

• • •

- 25 -

If you hire the wrong guy, you now have two problems: the original problem, and now you've got a guy to fire.

Let's be clear about why you hire people: to solve a problem—your problem. Hiring them to solve their problem is not business, but charity. Don't get me wrong, we have obligations and opportunities to be charitable, and a good person gives generously. But be honest about what you're doing, and don't call it a business transaction. That's only going to lead to frustration on everyone's part when it is inevitably revealed that you have an employee or contractor who costs money but brings no value to the business.

If you do have a problem to solve and you hire the wrong person—whether out of carelessness, charity, or an honest mistake—you actually double your trouble. The thing you needed fixed is still broken, and you have a contractor or employee that you have to separate from. That takes time, energy, and (increasingly) money. It also involves risk, and you've lost time and opportunities while you had the round peg in the square hole.

So when you hire, make sure that it's clear in your own mind what you need done. You can't communicate expectations to an employee or contractor if you don't understand them yourself. As they say in carpentry, measure twice and you only have to cut once.

If you do end up with the wrong person, don't let a bad situation fester. Yes, people can grow into their roles, and it's in your best interests to help develop your team. But a poor fit doesn't fix itself. It takes time and energy to make it better. You must address the problem when it's clear that there is problem. If you don't, the wound will get infected, and the remedies are going to be more painful and costly.

The wise, good, and free person manages business relationships with care and tends to what needs tending. Anything else is foolish, unfair to everyone involved, and enmeshes you in bad contracts.

• • •

- 26 -

Charisma without character is a prescription for disaster. Someone is going to get hurt. Lovable rogues make great movie characters, but in real life they leave damage in their wake.

Charisma is hard to define. The dictionary tells us that it is a special magnetic charm or appeal, especially a personal magic of leadership arousing loyalty or enthusiasm among followers. But what are the components? Good looks? Wit? Talent? Great communication skills? The list could go on, but none of those is sufficient to explain why some people have charisma and some don't. It is not something that you can articulate, but something that you feel at a visceral level when you meet some people.

The dictionary is right: charisma is magnetic. It draws us to some people, and if it's strong enough we will follow them almost anywhere. A charismatic leader can cause armies to march, explorers to plunge into the unknown, nations to commit atrocities, investors to lose their life savings, and cultists to commit mass suicide. Charisma can override wisdom, goodness, and freedom. Under its spell, we will do foolish things, knowing they are foolish; we will surrender our virtue and decency; we will give up our liberty.

This is why character matters in a leader. In our culture, it's becoming more popular to say that the private lives and morals of our political leaders are irrelevant. All that matters is their brand, their message, and the charisma they have to sell it. Wise, good, and free people (that want to stay that way) will recognize that the more charismatic a leader is, the more reason to check for character. We do not want this powerful force wielded by a fool, a bad man, or someone who does not cherish our freedom.

• • •

- 27 -

Slavery was a screwed up idea. But admitting that only makes it more puzzling. We need to understand how something so screwed up could have happened. Because if we could understand that, we would learn a lot about ourselves and this world. What screwed up injustice are we overlooking today that will baffle everyone a century or two from now?

• • •

- 28 -

No matter how old you get, never stop being childlike. But please stop being childish as soon as possible.

Aspire to be forever young.

We cannot stop our bodies from aging, but the best of our humanity is lost when our hearts and minds grow old. Even Jesus said that we must receive the Kingdom of God like a child.

But child*like* is not the same as being child*ish*. The first is what Jesus was talking about; the second is not the way of wisdom, goodness, and freedom. What are the differences?

Childlike people set out with innocent motives, but also have the self-awareness to recognize when other motives taint their original intentions. And they are capable of feeling guilty when they are wrong, of saying they are sorry and really meaning it. Childish people insist on their own innocence, because they are incapable of seeing themselves or their actions from anyone else's point of view. They are never genuinely sorry for wrongdoing, although they are often sorry that they got caught.

Childlike people are honest and open. Years of conflict have not left layers of emotional scar tissue, defensiveness, and deception. They can share feelings with other people. Childish people are merely indiscrete. Their emotions are so close to the surface that they blurt things out and damage those around them. They lack the ability to self-edit.

Childlike people are humble. They know when they have done a good job, but they don't boast and rub it in and seek advantage over others. Childish people cycle back and forth, sometimes over the course of a few minutes, between arrogance and self-loathing. Childish people see every relationship as a dramatic scene where they must be either the hero or the victim.

Childlike is spontaneous. Childish is undisciplined.

Childlike is trusting. Childish is gullible.

Childlike is simple. Childish is simple-minded.

Childlike people are sometimes ignorant, but eager to learn. Childish people are foolish, uncurious, and incapable of heeding correction.

The childlike person looks to the future, open to possibility. The childish person yearns for yesterday's pleasures and nurses old grudges.

Let us strive to be wise, do good, and live free—with young souls and childlike joy.

• • •

- 29 -

The news media compresses time and space, so that it seems that the whole world is on fire, held hostage, sliding into the sea, or blowing up. It isn't. Stop staring at the screen, walk outside, and look around. The world is bigger and better in person than on TV.

• • •

- 30 -

Any ordinary morning might turn into an extraordinary day. Be prepared.

Moses was eighty years old, tending sheep around the slopes of a dusty mountain in the Sinai desert. It was like any other morning, until he rounded a corner and saw a bush that was burning, but not consumed. His life, and the lives of millions (and billions to come), would never be the same.

Some sailors were in their bunks with hangovers, some sat in chapel, some drank coffee while doing crossword puzzles, and some were AWOL, spending time with ladies who were not their wives, when the bombs fell on a Sunday morning at Pearl Harbor.

People in the World Trade Center were doing their jobs, eating their bagels, fighting with their spouses on the phone, goofing off on the Internet, waiting for an elevator, and silently passing gas in the lobby while keeping a straight face when the first plane hit.

We can't catalogue all the ordinary mornings throughout history that were interrupted by earthquakes, unexpected opportunities, car accidents, pregnancy tests, heart attacks, or letters containing life-changing news.

We wake up, do our morning ritual in the bathroom, eat some breakfast, and begin going about our day. It might be routine, or it might be a day when we are distracted and stressed. Regardless, when we are looking to our right, something can hit us from our blind spot on the left. Before you are done reading this page, your world might change.

We can't make life more predictable. But the wise, good, and free person can make it more survivable by preparing for what can be anticipated, being rooted in values that endure whatever is thrown at them, and cultivating flexibility and resilience.

● ● ●

- 31 -

No matter how advanced our technology is, we still depend on people who can build and fix and fight. We who cannot do these things shouldn't be so stupid and suicidal as to despise the people who can.

Some people like to say that the United States has evolved into a "creative economy." By that, they mean that we don't manufacture a lot of things, but we invent them, and new ways to use them. So, for example, the MacBook Air I'm typing this on was invented in Cupertino, but manufactured in China, and I'm using it to write a book, which will be sold on Amazon.com, a company that has created a new kind of relationship between writers and readers.

Fair enough. But while I have no idea what percentage of Americans make their living in the "creative economy" (I count myself blessed to be one of them), I suspect that it isn't more than ten percent or so. It is, however, the ideal for those who work in it, and many who aspire to. We feel liberated, enlightened, and evolved. We are much cleverer than the uncreative types. Yeah us!

Be Wise, Do Good, Live Free

Far more Americans work in government and service jobs. They teach school or work in restaurants or retail stores. But in their free time they surf on their smart phones, and aspire to do something creative. Lots of us want to live in gleaming cities full of smart electronics powered by clean energy, surrounded by flat screens suggesting brands to our hungry consumer dreams. Few of us want to do something dirty or dangerous, see anything dirty or dangerous, or be reminded that all of this only exists because some people do things that are dirty or dangerous.

But we want our devices to power up. We want our heating and air conditioning to work every time. We want our planes to stay in the air and our poop to flush away, never to be seen again. We want the seas to be safe and tourists not to be kidnapped or blown up in some equatorial resort.

All of these things require people who can do more than type on a MacBook, or build websites, or pick interior colors. Our creative economy rests on those who can build and fix and fight. We had better not despise them. Not because they might revolt, but because we need more of them. If we don't honor what they do, our kids will continue to aspire to doing anything except building, fixing, and fighting. Then they'll be importing guest workers to keep the power on and the poop flushing while we sit in coffee houses and play games on iPhones paid for by government benefits. We'll become what large swaths of Europe have become. That is not a stable or prosperous future.

• • •

- 32 -

Ambition can blind us to opportunity. Ambitions are the supply side of life's economy: they are what we want to give to (or in some cases push upon) the world. Opportunities are what the world wants or needs from us.

Supply-side creativity is a magical thing, beautiful to watch. A great inventor imagines some wonderful new thing and delivers it to the world like Prometheus bringing fire to mankind in Greek mythology. Steve Jobs of Apple and Jeff Bezos of Amazon are recent models of the ideal.

But most successful people are demand-driven, including most of the great inventors and innovators. They see the wants and needs around them, listen to what people are asking for, and figure out how to make and deliver it.

They have an uncanny instinct for finding and figuring out opportunities. They see gaps and shortcomings, the frustrations or unfilled expectations of people or businesses. Read a book on the history of invention and you realize that many of the greatest products and companies in history were not conceived by someone accidentally spilling a beaker in a lab and discovering some new Wonder Thing. Instead, someone was trying to solve a problem that everyone else was aware of and working on. Often, they went through countless possible solutions that didn't work before they hit on the right combination that did. After that, ambition kicked in as they came up with a plan to sell it into the marketplace.

The same can be said for careers. Some people do form an early dream to grow up and be something and work relentlessly at it. Some careers pretty much require an early ambition because the education and training is so long and selective and expensive: doctors and fighter pilots, for example. One doesn't stumble into being a brain surgeon at forty-two years old by responding to an advertisement online.

The wise, good, and free person pays careful attention to what others want and need, and is shrewd, inventive, and hard-working enough to meet some of them. That's how they get ahead. If you want to succeed, focus less on your ambitions, and pay more attention to opportunities.

• • •

- 33 -

Just because you can doesn't mean you should. Much wisdom is contained in that sentence, and much grief can be avoided if you live by it. Freedom won't last if it isn't exercised with wisdom and goodness.

• • •

- 34 -

Every art form has a purpose. Music has charms to sooth the savage beast and a picture is worth a thousand words, right? But some ideas can only be unpacked with tens of thousands of carefully chosen words. If you don't read books, whole worlds will be forever out of your reach.

Admittedly, since I'm in the book business, I'm prejudiced on this point. But bias aside, I'm sure that I'm right: we need books. They might be the classic dead-tree models (paper) or nothing but ones and zeros that rearrange themselves into pixels on a screen, but we cannot do without books.

A book is the right tool for certain jobs. In fiction, no movie can ever explore the complexity of a world or the depth of a character like a novel can. Films are no less creative, but they are creative in a different way. They use different arts to achieve a different end.

Books that introduce ideas have changed the world. With tens of thousands of words a book has the luxury of breaking down a problem, seeing it from multiple angles, exploring and testing solutions. Afterward, the concept might be reduced to a video, an article online, or into a speech. But those are derivatives and summaries. You cannot engage with the concept from a summary. Not to mention that you are captive to whoever is doing the summarizing.

Wise, good, and free people produce a literate society. It's not a coincidence that liberty, invention, and prosperity correlate with literacy rates. Historically, cultures that read and treasure books have outpaced cultures that do not by every conceivable measure. Genuinely literate cultures don't hold books as mere ideals, to be read by a few scholars at the top of the social pyramid. When Guttenberg's press and Tyndale's translation of the scriptures allowed every English plowboy read the Bible, it changed England and the world. The Dutch traders and the American soldiers who traveled the world with books in their packs did more to spread the virtues of civilization and freedom than all the Spanish conquistadors or Japanese soldiers/wanna-be Samurai ever could.

Big ideas are powerful things, and they need a big platform to unfold themselves on. Let us never stop being a People of the Book.

• • •

- 35 -

Civilization paid for some lessons with blood. Unfortunately, we keep having to pay the tuition over and over again with the same mistakes every generation.

• • •

- 36 -

Be careful choosing who you love, because love is a choice. And then love the one you have chosen, because love is a commitment.

We treat love as if it were a condition that comes upon us, not a conscious choice—as if one walks along, minding one's own business, when one is surprised by Cupid's arrow and is afflicted with love, powerless in its grasp. It's as if love were merely a noun, the verb were something like struck/captured/enchanted/infected, and the direct object were me. In that sentence, love did something to me. I am the passive object of its power.

I'm sorry, but I don't buy it. I may be attracted to someone (for a variety of reasons), but I love them. I am the subject, love is the verb, and the direct object is the other person. Love is something that I do, not a thing that affects me. I realize that we can't always control our emotions, but love is the choice to open the floodgate of our emotions and let it flow onto someone.

We should be very careful about who we choose to direct our love toward. As someone has pointed out, *Romeo and Juliet* is not really a great romantic example of the power of love: it's the story of a couple of fourteen-year-olds who lose control of their hormonal urges, and over three days six people die. This should not be a model for…well, for anything. But over the millennia, men and women (and boys and girls) have chosen to love foolishly, and thus have lost both their goodness and freedom.

Love shouldn't make us fools, strip us of our virtue, and make us lose our liberty. Yes, that's what the poems and songs and plays tell us. And that's certainly what has happened over and over again throughout the human experience. But that same experience, the wealth of the generations, warns us over and over not to repeat the mistake. You can throw up your hands and cry, "I can't resist any better than millions before me," but the wise, good, and free person at least tries. Recognize the power of attraction, but master the verb of love. Perhaps only the unwise use of money has ruined more lives than poorly chosen love.

But once you have chosen whom you will love, commit yourself to him or her. To love is not to always feel attracted (that's the difference between love and emotional attraction), but to serve another person. Our wedding vows should be seriously considered and once given, taken seriously.

• • •

- 37 -

We have moved death too far away from our daily lives.

Most people who have lived on this earth were familiar with death. Grandma died in the next room. Brothers and sisters died. Women died in childbirth. There were wars and plagues. Villages and neighborhoods had little cemeteries that we passed by every day, with fresh flowers on the tombstones. Churchyards always included graveyards, so we thought about death and the Bigger Story as we walked through them into the sanctuary.

In modern America, we've moved all of that as far away as possible. People die in hospitals, or perhaps in hospice facilities, but rarely at home. The bodies are whisked away by professionals, and even the open casket at the funeral home is a brief, stylized experience. In fact, I'm surprised by how few funerals most of us have been through.

Don't get me wrong: it's not a bad thing that mortality rates are lower than they used to be and that we don't have siblings and neighbors dropping from influenza or smallpox. Literally, we should thank God and the amazing powers of modern medicine.

But people still die (all of us do, in fact), and I do wonder whether it's a good thing that we so rarely journey inside a hospice to visit the dying, or a graveyard to reflect on the how brief our stories are and just how long the Big Story that runs through the generations is. Very little of what happens to us is original, because so many have had the same joys and heartaches throughout the long generations. At the time we have to experience these things goes by so quickly. Which is all the more reason we should learn from those who have come before, and give to those who come after. We can inherit wisdom, goodness, and freedom, or we can squander these gifts that our ancestors earned the hard way.

• • •

- 38 -

Wannabe warriors boast and pose and taunt. True warriors, the real deal, never brag or strike a pose. Their language is either self-controlled respect, or focused, purposeful violence.

I am not a pacifist. There is a place for armed conflict. Not all wars are just, but there are just wars. We shouldn't start unjust wars (although we may need to defend ourselves when they are launched upon us). All of that can (and should) be debated.

But one thing is clear to me: there are a few real warriors, and lots of (mostly) guys who want to be warriors, but actually aren't. The posers prance and preen and pretend. They show off their weapons, shooting them pointlessly in the air in third world conflict zones for cameramen who broadcast it to gullible populations in comfortable countries who haven't seen a war in a generation. They swoon with delight or fear (depending on the politics of everyone involved) at these idiots wasting ammunition.

The real warriors that took Omaha Beach or defended Bastogne the next Christmas, or the professional operators who have waged firefights in the dark behind enemy lines that will never be written about, or the brilliant and brave who drive some of the most complex machines ever built above the clouds or below the waves—these men and women don't brag or boast, award themselves with ridiculous ranks or fake medals, or dress like action heroes when they are not in action. They are self-controlled, of above average intelligence, well trained, respectful, and they don't enjoy violence. They are not teenagers playing a video game nor are they untrained young men in a gang or third world army who use their soldiery as an opportunity to bully and steal and rape. They are prepared to rapidly unleash extreme, lethal violence on anyone and anything they are ordered to attack. But when the mission is accomplished, they just want to go home.

A wise, good, and free nation needs wise, good, and free men and women to fight for it when necessary. That is how liberty is preserved in a world with plenty of foolish, evil, armed enemies. We should honor and support the real warriors that allow us to sleep safely in our beds at night.

• • •

- 39 -

Beware living in a bubble with people who kiss your butt. Who is telling you the truth?

The dictionary defines *sycophant* as: "A servile self-seeker who attempts to win favor by flattering influential people."

The world is full of sycophants. If you've enjoyed any success at all, if you are one of those "influential people" the dictionary mentions, you have sycophants around you. The higher you climb, the more they attach themselves to your underside, like remoras on a shark.

If successful, influential, and powerful people are not careful, eventually they come to live in an alternative reality, a bubble whose mirrored walls reflect inward. Egged on by the sycophants around them, they bask in the reflected glory of their own self-image. It never occurs to them that the sycophants have an agenda, that they all want something.

It's fun to be flattered. It's delightful to have people tell you how delightful you are. It confirms what you have always known about yourself but were too modest to mention in public. Your mother was right: you are special!

You may not be a president or rock star. But that doesn't mean you don't have sycophants. The people who work for you want their paychecks, and they probably want your job. The salespeople who call on you don't really find you as fascinating as they seem to; they want you to sign on the dotted line. The students who gush about your lectures want a grade, the parishioners who gush about your sermons want your attention, and the guys who nod their heads while listening to stories about your exploits to find new shoes at the mall want…well, you figure that out.

The wise, good, and free person makes sure they have someone who tells them the truth about who they are.

• • •

- 40 -

If there is something that really needs to be done, then stop reading about wisdom, be wise. Go do it. Now. I'll wait (I'm only a book, I'm not going anywhere).

• • •

- 41 -

We are created with equal humanity, dignity, and worth. But, of course, we are not created with equal abilities or even opportunities. We can do our best to make life "fair," but the outcomes will never turn out even. But each of us should have as much freedom as possible to play our hand with wisdom and goodness.

One of the reasons that life is not "fair" is that there so many ways in which we are not equal. We are not created equal in intellect, stature, running speed, vocal cords, hair color, breast size, or any number of other things. Nor do we all have equal opportunities. Some of that is an indictment of social injustices, but some of it just life. Some of us had bad parents, suffered childhood illnesses, or had a tornado tear through our town.

We are equal in inherent dignity and worth, which means we deserve life, liberty, and the opportunity to pursue happiness. We should have equal protection under the law and be addressed with equal respect by our government.

But even if we are given opportunities as equal as they can be this side of heaven, there has never been a society that produced equal results. However the game is set up and played, some will come out ahead. The gun fires and the race of life begins. And although we may not all get the same number of days, we do all get the same number of hours in the day. Even in communist paradises (like...?), some use their hours more wisely, some will do more good for themselves and others, and some will remain free from debt, drugs, and dumb relationships.

And this means there will be always be an unequal distribution of all sorts of things: grades in the classroom, goals on the soccer field, the attention of the opposite sex, job offers, admiration of peers, children who turn out OK. Not to mention the more obvious and tangible measures of success, like money.

The wise, good, and free person has no fear of a meritocracy. They may not win every contest, but they do well and know that their rewards are just. It is the foolish, evil, and unfree that always want to rig the game somehow.

• • •

- 42 -

They say that you learn more from losing than winning. Maybe, sometimes. But if you're not careful, you only learn how to lose.

Whenever we lose, someone tries to make us feel better by telling us how much we must have learned from the experience. And they can be right. We can learn from losing. But we don't automatically learn anything from a loss; losing itself imparts no wisdom.

Losing can teach us humility, but not necessarily. Some people are so proud and arrogant that they can't accept any responsibility for a loss. It doesn't humble them, it makes them indignant. They fancy themselves a victim, or even a martyr, whose deserved victory was stolen from them. Some have an elevated sense of self-esteem that is weirdly disconnected from any actual ability or accomplishment. Losing doesn't make them feel bad or humbled since success isn't the source of their self-esteem.

Some people become comfortable with losing and come to accept it as normal. Their sense of self-worth may go down, but not always. They just become convinced that victory is a low-percentage phenomenon and become comfortable with mediocre performance. At least that's how I have come to look at my golf game.

For losing to have value, we must undertake the effort to understand why we lost. If that post-mortem examination leads us to reevaluate our abilities and our pride in them, then it can be a humbling experience. If we then use that to constructively improve ourselves or improve our odds for success next time by competing on our strengths, then losing might be very instructive. If our analysis shows us critical errors that caused the loss and we make the effort to correct those for next time, then a loss might lead to a later victory.

But if we are not careful, losing becomes a disease. Loss breeds loss, until we become numb to failure. We don't evaluate afterwards, we don't learn or grow, or try harder next time. We just shrug and accept our lot. That is neither wise, nor good, and it doesn't lead to freedom.

• • •

- 43 -

You don't always have to invent a better mousetrap to succeed in business. You can just do a better job selling regular mousetraps.

We've all heard that the way to succeed in business is to invent a better mousetrap. And some business owners despair, because they aren't that inventive.

But we don't necessarily need to invent a different kind of mousetrap, some revolutionary concept that reinvents the relationship between mouse, man, and death. You don't need to be Steve Jobs and come up with the iTrap.

You can do very well in business making regular old mousetraps, but making them better, or cheaper, or delivering them faster, or getting them to distant markets where they've never heard of mousetraps, or selling them with a smile so that your customers love and are loyal to you. You could offer to bait them for your customers or come to their house to dispose of the dead mice. The combinations for success with the venerable mousetrap design are endless.

Consider the humble haircut. As near as I can tell, no one has invented a new way to cut hair in quite some time. But it seems like there's a haircut place on every corner in my town. Why? Well, (almost) everyone needs his or her hair cut. There's a big market to share, but they don't really compete by offering a different product. They all offer essentially the same product. They differ slightly on quality, service, price, convenience, and amenities, whatever. Some will tell you that they have a better mousetrap because they've radically reinvented the hair cutting experience. Whatever. Look, there are better and worse haircuts, but they are still just haircuts.

My point is this: don't beat yourself up if you can't be Steve Jobs and invent the iTrap or some other new clever widget. I've reached the place in life where I'm comfortable and content buying from certain businesses, not because they do something different, but because they do something better. I have my favorite coffee shop, my favorite lawn care guy, and my favorite haircut place.

The wise, good, and free businessperson can find plenty of ways to succeed by being shrewd, decent, and keeping his or her business free of debt and bad relationships.

• • •

- 44 -

Let your faith shape your ideology. Don't let your politics choose your religion. The abuses of religion are usually not from an excess of spirituality, but from a lack of it. In history's worse cases, religion was dragged in to justify what worldly people wanted to do anyway.

• • •

- 45 -

Conspiracy theories rest on several premises, one of which is that people can keep their mouths shut. Nothing in history suggests that this is possible.

From the Illuminati to Roswell to 9/11, all conspiracy theories require us to believe that:

- A large number (often a vast network, sometimes multi-generational) of highly intelligent people have engaged in complex operations (often over vast distances, in disconnected organizations) to carefully coordinate something that has no clearly defined purpose and has largely failed to achieve whatever goals they supposedly do have. But they are working to achieve their "ends," even if they will never live to see them.
- They have coordinated this effort over many years, decades, or centuries by communicating somehow through some method that has left no demonstrable trace of documents, records, recollections, or witnesses. Others (not clear if these others are part of the conspiracy) have cooperated in suppressing this evidence.
- All the people involved (numbers usually run into the thousands or more) have kept their mouths shut, even to their dying days, because they were True Believers in the Cause, or because they were paid well enough to ensure

their lifetime of silence, or they were afraid of Them and the consequences of speaking out.

Nothing in human experience suggests that anything like this is possible. No one keeps secrets. Conspiracy theorists say that commitment to the cause, money, or fear has bought silence. Really? Simple observation tells us that people are blabbermouths, and everything eventually leaks. Especially if it's juicy gossip and someone could get rich or famous for by spilling the beans.

Occam's Razor never dulls over time: the simplest explanation for anything is still the best. If you hear a stampede of approaching hoofs, it's probably not zebras (unless you are on Serengeti Plain, or wherever zebras live).

The wise, good, and free person doesn't waste his or her time on conspiracy theories. They are usually a rationalization to avoid an uncomfortable truth, or entertainment for weak minds that won't constructively engage with a reality they want to avoid.

• • •

- 46 -

We modern people love nature because we don't have to face it in its raw form. Our ancestors endured it without all the technology that lets us enjoy its charms while keeping dry, warm, fed, and safe. It terrified them.

• • •

- 47 -

Don't make excuses. But you may owe some people explanations.

There's a big difference between excuses and explanations. Excuses try to justify mistakes and bad behavior. The premise of an excuse is that while we may have done something wrong, we weren't wrong. It wasn't our fault, somehow, and we shouldn't be blamed for the outcome. Excuses seem slippery; they are a dishonest attempt to dodge responsibility and to deflect fair criticism. Excuses are not wise, because they are annoying, transparent, and we lose respect and credibility every time we make them. Excuses are not good, because they are dishonest, serve no one but ourselves, and don't make the world a better place. And while we might make excuses in an attempt to get out of trouble, they don't set us free because we become trapped by lies and unintended consequences.

But the wise, good, and free person realizes that he or she may owe people explanations for mistakes, failures, and wrongdoings. An explanation is honest about what happened, and it doesn't try to shift blame or evade responsibility. An explanation helps everyone grow, because when we understand why something happened, we have more power to prevent it from happening again. An explanation is liberating, because it defuses tension, restores broken relationships, and accepts consequences so that we can move on to a better future.

• • •

- 48 -

Worry about money pierces the heart, corrodes the mind, and makes the taste of life sour. It leads to all sorts of grief and evil. So figure it out, and relieve your stress. Find ways to lower your overhead, earn more, spend less, save more, and want less. Give more. Figure it all out so that you can live as freely as possible.

There is a common misunderstanding that the Bible says that money is the root of all evil. That's obviously not true, and the actual quote is much more accurate and chilling. It's in 1 Timothy 6, verses 9-10:

> *Those who want to get rich fall into temptation and a trap and into many foolish and harmful desires that plunge people into ruin and destruction. For the love of money is a root of all kinds of evil. Some people, eager for money, have wandered from the faith and pierced themselves with many griefs.*

We will always have to exchange goods and services, whether it is by bartering or exchanging hard currency. And there will never be enough stuff or power to fill the bottomless pit of our desires. There is nothing wrong with trying to make money, but the quest to succeed is a minefield with a thousand hidden perils. Financial stress will rot you from the inside out.

Don't let that happen. Since the problem attacks from every side, you have to solve it from every angle. Don't spend more than you earn, but earn as much as you can while being faithful to your dreams, values, and commitments. Put money aside for a rainy day, but be generous and don't be pennywise and pound-foolish. Beware of debt, for nothing else has more consistently enslaved people throughout history. Be wise and good with money, and stay free.

• • •

- 49 -

When you speak a word of wisdom to someone, do it to build them up not to tear them down. The purpose of wisdom is always to make life bigger and better, not smaller and worse.

• • •

- 50 -

Failure can be generational. Set your children free from your foolishness and sin. Give them liberty by teaching them to be wiser and better than you are.

If a child learns to work hard, manage his or her money, be honest, moral, and kind to others, then they will not be surprised when people expect those things of them as an adult.

And yet, too many parents and teachers indulge their children, setting them up to fail when they get out of the protective custody of their extended adolescence. These kids grow up to resent the lifestyle of their wise, good, and free neighbors who are more successful than they are. They whine about "unfair" standards, or suspect that the "system" has been rigged to discriminate against them and favor a privileged few. Because they were never taught to connect their character or actions to outcomes, or that they had the ability to do better by being better people, they cannot accept personal responsibility for their lives. Even that last sentence offends them: *what do you mean, "better people?" Where do you get off saying some people are better? Do you think that you are better than me?*

Of course, we can all be better people. We can be better educated, better workers, better housekeepers, better managers of our money, better parents, and better friends. We can improve ourselves by learning to speak a foreign language, typing faster, having less body fat and more endurance, using our time more wisely to accomplish more, being more generous, speaking more kindly to others, whatever.

Take the examples in the last paragraph, and add any others that you can think of. Now ask yourself, if we are not better by all those measures but worse, then what do we pass on to our children? If our lives are marked by foolishness, incompetence, laziness, poor judgment, bad relationships, addictions, debt, unhealthy habits and abuse of our bodies, sexual irresponsibility, dishonesty, anger, jealousy, resentment, inflated self-esteem, feelings of unjustified entitlement and victimhood, and general moral decay—then I guarantee you two things. You are probably not succeeding in life. You might have idiot savant-like success in one area because of some singular talent (you're a pro athlete, actor, or rock star, or you're a mathematical genius who can pick stocks or count cards), but if it were not for that big pole in the middle then the rest of your life would be a collapsed tent.

The second thing I'm sure of is this: you are passing your failures on to your children. They are learning from you to be foolish, bad, and enslaved. They will grow up to elect leaders who promise to make life "fair" by tearing down and taking away from the wise, good, and free who have chosen and enjoy better lives. That is where we are headed as a nation, as the failures of the fathers are being visited upon the children unto the third and fourth generation, just like the Bible promised.

• • •

- 51 -

You don't succeed by working hard but by producing results. Good results almost always come from hard work, but working hard doesn't always produce results. People who work hard with no results often resent their lack of success. Work both hard and smart.

When we were kids, we were rewarded for effort. That's the way it should be, because the point of the lesson is to teach good work habits, persistence, responsibility, etc. But somewhere in our upbringing and education, there needs to be a transition where we start rewarding performance. That's the way it worked until a few generations ago: somewhere around the end of elementary school we stopped getting graded for effort and not everyone got to play on the sports team. Grades and goals measured the quality of our performance, not the quantity of our effort.

Our educational and parenting standards have slipped, and the result is not producing a more egalitarian society of equal outcomes. In fact, it is backfiring and producing income gaps and class divisions. Why? Because some people have figured out that results do matter in the real world, and some have not.

In the real world, no one cares how hard you worked on that product, or that house, or that meal. If your product isn't good, consumers won't buy it. If your home repairs are shoddy and ugly, no one will pay top dollar for them. If your food is bad and overpriced, your restaurant will fail. Socialists will come along and promise you that they will use the coercive power of the government to level outcomes, like some self-esteem sports camp where there are no losers, only winners, and everyone gets a participants ribbon. Some mediocre performers will always demand "fairness," and there will always be some politician promising to deliver it through the force of law or the barrel of a gun. But such states always fail, because it's a fantasy that runs against the grain of reality.

Every wise, good, and free person I have ever met works incredibly hard. But they work that hard to produce great results, knowing that they will be measured by their results. They never resent someone else getting rewarded because they performed better than they did. The wise, good, and free work hard and smart.

• • •

- 52 -

Originality is overrated. A good idea isn't good just because it's new. I'll take a good, old idea any day instead of having something foolish or bad shoved down my throat just because it's original.

• • •

- 53 -

Revolutions almost never lead where the revolutionaries imagined. When a system is torn down, the law of unintended consequences runs wild—for better and worse. Wise, good, and free people think before they unleash revolutionary change, and they take responsibility for the outcomes.

Don't misunderstand me: change is inevitable, and revolutions can be great things. But they aren't always great things, even if they begin with great intentions.

A revolution is not the same as redecorating your house. Corporations, cultures, and countries are complex systems. They have lots of moving parts, and those gears mesh with all the systems around them. When you redecorate your home, you are coping with half a dozen variables—in the worst-case scenario you can just put it back like it was. But when you turn over a society or a nation, you unleash thousands of variables, most of which you don't even know about. The ball bounces in ways you never imagined it could, and things get out of your control very quickly.

That is not to say we don't need revolutions. At times, they are the least-worst alternative and a necessary, calculated risk. But a commitment to wisdom, goodness, and freedom dictates a high threshold to justify revolutionary change. The French Revolution of 1789 and the Soviet Revolution of 1917 were both made up of angry, hungry, resentful mobs stirred up by opportunistic revolutionaries that would soon become brutal dictators. History is full of such examples, glorious revolutions dedicated to high ideals that made countries worse (at least in the short run), not better. Sober men, who thought long and hard about the potential consequences, took the risk anyway and launched the American Revolution of 1776. Even so, it led to unintended consequences, like structurally prolonging slavery for almost another century, until another failed revolution (the Civil War) forced the question.

We should not be afraid of change, but we have a responsibility to our own generation and those ahead to make it as small as possible to achieve our ends.

• • •

- 54 -

The purpose of a business is not to create jobs, but to make a profit. On the balance sheet, workers are a cost, not an asset. Job creation is a consequence of profitable growth. Workers who forget this will get disappointed, owners who forget this will go broke, and governments who ignore this will make everyone poorer.

• • •

- 55 -

The Law of Entropy means that leaders can't be merely caretakers. They must put energy and effort into their organization or it will fall apart. Nothing runs itself.

The Law of Entropy is the popular name for the Second Law of Thermodynamics. What it amounts to, for our purposes, is this: order and structure gradually break down as the energy that holds things together dissipates into the surrounding environment. So, for example, your hot cup of coffee becomes colder as the heat escapes through the cup into the air around it. Your office or your house becomes messy as the energy it takes to maintain it is spent on other activities. The money in your bank account dribbles out as your bills come due.

Leaders need to be keenly aware of the problem of entropy. Things fall apart, including organizations, unless you either constantly put energy into them or vacuum-seal and deep freeze them. And since the second option is pointless and impossible anyway, that leaves leaders stuck with the first: they must constantly put energy into their organization and their leadership of it.

If you ignore your business, your team, your church, or your family, they will begin to fall apart. The energy of the organization will leak out through a thousand little holes. There will always be something that tempts, distracts, or diffuses the attention and order of the organization. You have to plug as many of those holes as you can, but you'll never get all of them. In addition to your constant plugging, you need to keep adding enough energy into the tank to make up for the seepage through the sides. That can't be only organizational carrots or sticks. It requires constant creative investment. Wise, good, and free leaders never deceives themselves by taking their leadership for granted; they serve what they lead by pouring themselves into it and never asking anyone to be more committed to success they themselves are as a leader.

• • •

- 56 -

Raise your children to be wiser, better, and more free than you are. But don't forget that a million words of wise instruction can be undone with a single act of foolishness in their eyes. Teach with your life, for wisdom is shared by example.

• • •

- 57 -

I keep hearing that communism is a great idea, except that it doesn't work in the real world. I'm pretty sure that's the very definition of a *bad* idea.

It's a predictable slogan on college campuses, and increasingly in many churches: communism describes an ideal system that just happens to be impractical and impossible to implement (at this time, but that won't stop someone from trying again soon).

Here's what (I think) people mean by that. They assume that "from each according to his ability, to each according to his need" would be the most virtuous possible organizing principle for a society. After all, isn't that how it is, or should be, in a family? And what is society but the great human family? They assume (or assert) that this is what Jesus, or Buddha, or whichever religious leader they follow, really meant, that this was the core of their *real* message, which has been obscured over the centuries.

Unfortunately, they say, human nature is too flawed, too sinful, to live by this virtuous rule. Our greed keeps us from working for the greater good and for those less capable than ourselves. And so, say the college students and the sympathetic Christians, if capitalist societies have proven more prosperous and resilient than communist or socialist experiments, it is only because capitalism is an evil system that is more aligned with our own worst impulses. Some go so far as to say that communist experiments have only failed because they weren't communistic enough, and that greedy interlopers and capitalist enemies sabotaged the purity of their experiment. They daydream about it being properly implemented by revolutionaries who would be smart and ruthless enough to stamp out the last vestigial artifacts of self-interest in the hearts of the masses.

There are so many things wrong with this line of argument that I can't begin to address them here. But here's one important point: leaders have a responsibility to propose solutions that work. Telling my employees that our business model is to lose a little bit on every sale but to make it up in volume is absurd. I don't deserve to run the company. And condemning a nation to poverty, enslavement, and diminished opportunity because of a social theory that has never worked anytime or anywhere is not compassionate. At best it is malpractice, at worst it is opportunistic manipulation by the elite who will have the privilege of assigning the work and handing out the goodies.

Historically, there is no contest: the most successful social model has always been for wise and good people to be as free as possible. It organizes society by virtue and merit, calling upon and rewarding the best parts of our nature.

• • •

- 58 -

I admire my friend who sticks with his wife, despite her many challenges. When I ask him why, he answers, "She's my wife." Enough said.

My friend's wife has debilitating, chronic illnesses that have limited her lifestyle for years. Of course, they have limited his life as well, but we all remember that part of the wedding vows about "sickness and health." You would wish that she compensated for diminished physical capacity with a sunny disposition and engaging personality. But that doesn't describe her either, if you know what I mean. She is an unhappy person with constant low-grade pain (that I suspect is mostly in her mind) who throws a wet blanket over almost any situation. Add to that the demands of making a living, maintaining a family, and paying the bills, and there's not too much in my friend's home life that is fun.

Why does he stay in the marriage? Because he promised to. It's not more complicated than that. We promise to love, honor, cherish, obey, and serve with our body and worldly goods—through changing seasons of poverty and wealth, sickness and health—until death do us part. Where is the escape clause in that deal? Included in the virtues of wisdom, goodness, and freedom are honesty, integrity, and faithfulness. Liberty does not mean we are free to break our promises.

• • •

- 59 -

We spend most of our time obsessing about the two things we have the least control over: the past and the future. We have no control over the past because it is has, well, past. As to the future, we can make plans and preparations, but in practice, we have very little control over what happens tomorrow. What we do have control over is the present. Here's what you can decide: what will you do with the next five minutes? How will you live from now until you go to sleep tonight?

Living in the present tense has a cumulative effect. Choose to do the right thing with the next hour. Repeat. Put twenty-four right hours together, and you have a worthwhile day. Repeat. Eventually, you end up with a right week (or a mostly right week). Weeks become months, months become years, and one day you'll look back on a life full of love and learning and liberty. But if you try and chart your life from where you stand, you'll get intimidated and frustrated. Life is too big, with far too many variables, for you to game it all out.

So start where you are. Make the next hour wise, good, and free.

• • •

- 60 -

It's better to have a good job and happy life in a bad place than to have a miserable life in a nice place.

It is tempting to live somewhere cool, whatever that means for you: the bright lights of a big city, a mountain town, or near the beach. But be careful about making your career choices based more on where you will live than what you will do when you get there. You might end up only miles away from cultural landmarks or dramatic coastlines, but broke, in a dead-end job, with stress breaking down your body and family. You might never have the time, money, or energy to enjoy all the delights around you. You won't be able to take pride in your postal code and tell yourself that it's worth it.

The wise, good, and free person keeps careful account of how he spends his days. Most of us spend most of our waking hours working—are those hours satisfying and rewarding? Do your circumstances allow you to fully develop your personal and professional potential? Is there genuine opportunity to become the person you aspire to be, or are you in a place in which the opportunities are great but blocked by too much competition? Can you be good and do good where you are, or do your circumstances grind you down, burning out love and happiness?

Find a place where you can live as wisely, as good, and as freely as possible. Even if it's not a prestigious place, make that your home. Grow, bear fruit, and harvest a happy life.

• • •

- 61 -

The Gettysburg Address would not have been a better speech if Lincoln had opened with a joke or thrown in some punchy anecdotes.

Somewhere in your career you might have the opportunity to give a speech. The very thought terrifies some people, but others seek the spotlight. Either way, if you do get up in front of a room, there will be plenty of people giving you advice about how to win the crowd.

Some of that advice will be good, but not all of it. Among the worst is this: always establish a jokey familiarity with your audience. Start by trying to get a laugh, the theory goes, and then use lots of homey, hokey stories. If you're using presentation slides or video, some will advise you to toss in some goofy graphics to lighten the mood. All of this is based on the rather questionable premise that if the audience sees you as a "regular person," just like them, they will trust you and listen to what you have to say.

On some occasions, this might make sense. At some events, you might be called on to lighten the mood, or establish rapport. But those are almost never ends, only means. Why are you at the front of the room in the first place? No one wants to waste their time listening to a speaker who is just like them. If you're just like them, why aren't they giving the speech?

Lincoln's Gettysburg Address is only 263 words. The entire text is carved in marble next to his statue in his memorial in

Washington D.C. There is not a joke in it. People looked up to Lincoln. They didn't want him to be just like them, they wanted him to know more than they did, to say something that made them wiser, better, and more free.

When and if you get the chance to speak, humor can be a powerful tool. But it's a means to communicate more effectively. The whole point of you being up there is that they expect that you know something that they don't, that you have something valuable to say. Don't waste their time and squander your credibility by weirdly trying to prove that you don't belong behind the podium in the first place.

• • •

- 62 -

Information is not the same as wisdom. Wisdom is information that you understand, that you can use, and that makes you wiser, better, and more free. Effective leaders know the difference, and strive to turn information into wisdom.

• • •

- 63 -

Business success requires relationships and trust. In the end, people do business with those that they know and like. And whenever money changes hands, there must be trust.

Technology can reduce a transaction to a click or a card swipe or allow us to communicate from vast distances. But a vast web of relationships and trust make those transactions or conversations possible.

Inventing a better mousetrap is all well and good. But do you want to get investors to help you build the mousetraps? Assemble and run Better Mousetrap, Inc.? Sell the mousetraps? Here's what you'll need to do: be likable, get to know lots of people, and earn their trust.

Cynics like to say that it's not what you know, but whom you know. Of course we can always point to examples of people with limited ability that rise far beyond their level of competence because of family connections or boot-licking. But we can just as easily find examples of those who crashed and burned when their basic incompetence or dishonesty caught up with them. And we can, I think, find far more examples of people whose success roughly correlated to their competence, effort, likeability, relational capacity, and trustworthiness. That's the normal pattern in a free market. It's only when our society becomes unwise, not good, and freedom is limited that the unlikeable and untrustworthy succeed through manipulation and corrupt connections.

• • •

- 64 -
Book learning isn't everything. But it's something.

Of course you can't learn everything from books or in a classroom. Who said that you could? Success requires innate abilities, instincts, experience, and street smarts. None of those come from a book, and very little of it can be taught.

But we go too far if we devalue education and the things that we can learn in books and classrooms. We can always find examples of a person who succeeds without a formal education, whose grasp of reading, writing, and arithmetic is shaky at best. And we can find plenty of examples of people with stagnant careers and empty bank accounts that can diagram a sentence, find Timbuktu on a map, and derive a quadratic equation.

But I'd rather not have to choose between those extremes. If I could, I'd be someone who learns from books and from experience. If I could, I'd be literate and savvy. If I could, I'd take advantage of every opportunity to learn, from every available source. I'd never stop learning.

One thing that I would never do, if I wanted to live a wise, good, and free life: mock or disparage the legitimate arts and sciences (use those street smarts to filter out the bogus stuff that clutters up the modern university). Western Civilization rose as far as it did because of an accumulated intellectual heritage. I wouldn't take on great leadership responsibilities or thrust myself into the spotlight if I hadn't mastered at least the basics of the wealth of the generations.

• • •

- 65 -

Perfectionists rarely win. Far too often, they end up being underachievers, because if they can't do something perfectly, then they won't do it at all. Winners know when something is good enough.

We love the idea of perfectionism: the image of the master craftsman with uncompromising integrity, relentlessly working the details until it is done exactly right.

But the real master craftsman is the one who knows when something is done well enough that he can release his project and move onto the next one. Don't get me wrong: his standards are high, but not at perfection. Perfection is an abstraction, a mathematical concept that doesn't translate to the real world. We can describe a perfect circle, but can we cook a perfect meal, or build a perfect house, or write a perfect novel? Can your house be perfectly clean, or can you raise perfect children, or can you come up with the perfect solution to a problem?

Perfectionists get stuck in a loop of effort and frustration, trying to make something perfect. They never turn out perfect work, because perfection is unattainable. And because they cannot recognize that what they've done is good enough for their purposes (even though the standards might be very high), they achieve very little. Usually, they get frustrated and walk away from what they are trying to do or refuse to try. But they don't let it go; it eats them up inside. They are not often happy people.

While the perfectionist miserably stews about the imperfections of the world and his inability to fix it, the winners have figured out how to get things done close enough to perfect in order to move on to their next challenge. They are wise enough to do it good enough, and thus they are free.

• • •

- 66 -

Be careful about who you are, because it is who you are becoming. The older you get, the more you become whatever you are now. Grumpy and tired young people become grumpy and tired old people. Optimistic young people who can't sit still keep going until they can't anymore.

• • •

- 67 -

Of course we should discriminate. Can you imagine going through life without discriminating, or a society without any discrimination whatsoever? It would lead to moral, and eventually to literal, anarchy. The real question is, "On what *basis* should we discriminate?"

Do you want to live in a society that has no distinction between truth and falsehood? Between cruelty and compassion? Between what is wise, good, and free and what is stupid, ugly and enslaving? I'm sure that I don't want to live in that kind of society, but I fear that I increasingly do. I won't discriminate by race, but I sure want to discriminate by behavior. I'm happy to have a neighbor who has different skin color or speaks a different mother tongue, but I don't want someone who will roast my dog in his yard on a spit, or expose himself to the neighborhood children.

We don't want to unjustly discriminate, and so we are losing our capacity to do so justly. Learn to recognize and choose what is worthy and beautiful, and reject what is not.

Wisdom, goodness, and freedom require you to engage with big ideas that are uncomfortable within our culture. What is good, and what is evil? What is just and beautiful, and what is ugly and unfair? What kind of people do we want to be and how should we live? As a society we keep trying to avoid these questions, but they will not go away.

Do not make the mistake of believing that all ideas are of equal value, that all art is equally worthwhile, and that all choices lead to the same result. Discriminate freely in favor of justice and beauty. Stand for goodness, and against evil.

• • •

- 68 -

You don't have to live like a hobbit or hippie, but make time and space for some green things in your life.

I love urban spaces, and all the perks and wonders of advanced technology. But we were formed from the dirt. We were created to live in and tend a garden. When our lifestyle becomes too disconnected from the earth and growing things, we forget who we are.

Arrange your life so that you can regularly touch plants. If necessary, go to a small park, or sit in your yard. When you can, go somewhere more open and wild. Walk across fields, and through the woods. Don't ride anything, walk. Stop and listen to the wind rustling through branches. Breathe out your CO_2, and inhale the fresh oxygen. Eat a snack, and walk some more. Pee behind a tree. Don't be weird. It's not about you, so don't do some goofy dance or project your egotistical fantasies onto nature. Be humble and quiet. Let yourself be shaped a little bit by the natural elements that have defined the lives of most of the people who have lived on this planet: weather and soil and growing things.

When you do, you will learn that there is more to the natural world than science can measure or that we can imagine. It is not worthy of our worship, but it deserves our respect and attention. We cannot understand ourselves apart from the Creation. Find a farm or trail, and you will find part of yourself.

• • •

- 69 -

When traveling abroad, try to avoid dressing as if you are going on a safari, climbing a mountain, or are on a hippie gypsy vision-quest (unless, of course, you are actually doing these things). As much as possible, dress like the locals. If they don't need a dozen Velcro pockets and survival footgear to ride the metro in their city, you probably don't either.

There are two problems with traveling abroad in the costume of whatever personal fantasy you are currently living within.

First, you look like an idiot.

Second, you never really engage with the place you are visiting. You bring your own agenda to the encounter. You are insisting on experiencing it as an outsider, from an artificial point of view. You are projecting your fantasies onto the place instead of looking and listening, and thus learning from it.

I've done a fair amount of traveling. On a long trip, I certainly can't pack as if I was at home there. I'm living out of a suitcase, and my clothes need to fit into it, as well as be easy to pack and clean. I can't take separate wardrobes for every environment and occasion I might encounter on my trip. I may have to carry some of my belongings with me all day. Personally, I insist on wearing comfortable shoes, because I do a lot of walking when I travel. But all that being said, it's my goal to experience the culture wherever I'm going, and part of that is dressing as the locals do, as much as possible.

Make it your goal to experience the places you visit as they are, not as you wish them to be. Encounter and engage a foreign place, don't pretend that you and it are something you are not.

• • •

- 70 -

Ministry would be a great job if you didn't have to deal with people. Being an author would be a wonderful life, if it weren't for all the writing. Teaching would be so satisfying, if it wasn't for the students. And owning a business would be so rewarding, if it wasn't for trying to figure out how to make more money than you spend every month.

I meet young people all the time that dream of having some sort of a job for the lifestyle they imagine comes with it, without thinking too much about the actual substance of that career. If you think of the substance of your work as nothing more than a means to an end, you are neither a craftsman nor an artist. At best you will tolerate your work as a chore; at worst you will come to despise it.

Do you want to be a mother? Then love wiping butts and tears, and the daily effort of shaping a selfish child into a productive and responsible adult. Don't fantasize about the prestige and money that comes with being a surgeon; love the discipline and demands of surgery. You think that it would be fun to own a company? Don't start one unless you really enjoy risk, stress, long hours, and attention to detail. You crave the glamour of being a top chef or author? You'd better crave standing all day long over a hot stove or sitting in front of a word processor that won't fill itself.

Love doing the work enough, and you might get to where you want to go. And even if you don't get there, you might actually enjoy the job.

Don't aspire to a position, aspire to the work.

• • •

- 71 -

Sometimes, we go halfway around the world to be charmed by qualities that we would despise in our hometown. Distance breeds exotic charm, familiarity does breed contempt. Do you know how good you have it at home?

• • •

- 72 -

If you are a leader, multiply your effectiveness by training apprentices. But remember that the goal is not to have apprentices, it is to release them.

If you are a leader, are you training your replacement?

Insecure and selfish leaders do not. It's all about them, and they are either threatened by the idea of someone learning to do what they do, or they don't care enough about the people they are leading to have a succession plan in case something happens to them.

Great leaders give themselves away. They share not only what they've learned to do, but also how they do it. They don't just have assistants, they also train apprentices. An apprentice is not just an underling: it is someone who is learning to be like the leader. They are learning what the leader knows and feels, and how they think and do what they do. The leader reproduces himself in the apprentice. He cares enough about the people he leads to multiply his effectiveness in others.

But do not mistake means and ends: there is no point in having apprentices for their own sake. From the beginning, the whole relationship is focused on the day when the apprentice leaves to become a master practitioner of his own. Therefore, apprenticeships should not last one day longer than they have to in order to achieve that goal. It might take three months or three years, but do not take on an apprentice if what you really want is an assistant or a flunky.

Whom are you teaching what you know and how to do what you do? And what will you do when they learn? This world needs more wisdom, goodness, and freedom. Share and release as much of it as you've got.

• • •

- 73 -

In Africa, women really do carry things on their heads: Tupperware tubs and boxes of all sorts of stuff, plastic laundry baskets full of groceries, big trays full of fruits or yams stacked carefully, big steel bowls full of bottles of water, even a single loaf of bread. In most of the rest of this world, this would never occur to anyone. Lesson: there's more than one way to get something from Point A to Point B.

OK, it's not only in Africa, but that's where you see it most these days. You certainly don't see it in North America, Europe, Japan, most of Asia or the Middle East. I'd seen it on TV and movies, but the first time I went to West Africa and took the cab from the airport, I saw dozens of women carrying stuff on their heads at the first intersection in the city. It wasn't just a movie cliché, like so many other images of Africa.

It's not intuitive, at least not to me (and most folks throughout the rest of the world). After I made this observation, a well-traveled friend argued with me that is was quite common and made perfect sense. I told her that I have never seen a woman with her hands full in Europe, the Americas, or East Asia pick up a box of cereal or bag of dog food and carry it to the check-out counter at the grocery store on her head. I have never seen a college student set her books on her head and walk to class.

But this is the point: there is no reason not to. After I got back from that trip, I read online about carrying things on your head. It turns out that there are perfectly good physiological reasons to carry weight aligned on top of the spinal cord instead of off to one side.

This is my point: just because it hasn't occurred to you, doesn't mean it's not a perfect solution to the problem. Be open to suggestions, and look for ideas in unlikely places.

• • •

- 74 -

Do you make things more or less complicated for the people around you? How you answer that question probably explains the number and quality of your relationships.

• • •

- 75 -

Do not be like the guy who stops me on the street and says, "Hey, I've got a truckload of sombreros in a parking lot around the corner."

"Sombreros?" I ask.

"Yeah, man, sombreros. Over a thousand of them. A whole truckload."

"You mean the big Mexican hats? With the pointy top and the wide brim?"

"You got it. Nice ones, too. With the zig-zaggy shiny piping and the little dingly-dangly balls hanging from the brim." He points down the block. "Just right around the corner. Let's go."

I am very confused. "Why?"

"So you can buy some, of course." He looks at me like I'm slow-witted. Maybe I am, because I'm still not getting it.

"No, why do you have a truckload of sombreros with little dangly balls?"

"Oh," he shrugs, as if the answer were obvious. "I was down in Tijuana, and a guy was selling the whole lot, including the truck. It seemed like a good idea."

I stare at him, hoping for a better explanation, but apparently none is forthcoming. "So, you want me to buy a sombrero?"

"Well, actually I was hoping you'd buy a couple hundred, at least."

I stare some more, hoping that this will make sense at some point, and wondering if it would be worth waiting for.

"Come on man. You've got to help me out. I've got a real problem."

"What sort of problem? What am I missing?"

He looks at me like I'm stupid. "My problem is that I bought a truckload of a thousand sombreros with dangly balls and I need some cash."

"Ah, now I get it," I say as I step around him and continue down the street, "but that is *your* problem, not mine."

If you start a business, sell something that solves your customer's problem. He will never buy to solve yours.

• • •

- 76 -

Marketers can sell you almost anything, including a truckload of sombreros, if they tell a good enough story about you.

Let's suppose a guy buys a truckload of sombreros with little dangly balls hanging from the brim. He's got a huge problem since all his cash is tied up in hats, and he needs you to solve that problem by buying at least one of them.

Unless you're an idiot or feel sorry for him, you will never buy one to solve his problem. That's why markets are efficient: resources are not distributed by need or to satisfy some scheme of "fairness." People spend their money based on rational self-interest. All those people making all those purchase decisions comprise "the invisible hand" of the marketplace, voting on which products and providers add the most value.

So what do you do if you're the guy with the sombreros?

Well, you could market them by telling a story, but not a story about the sombreros, because you can't construct a narrative compelling enough to move a sombrero. Instead, the clever marketer will tell a story about the potential customer as the protagonist, with the sombrero as a character. Something like this:

"Hey man, are you OK?" says a guy, standing under an awning in front of a building downtown on a hot, summer day.

"Who, me?" you reply, looking around. "Sure, I'm fine, why do you ask?"

"Your face is looking a little flushed and blotchy. And you're walking a little wobbly."

"No, I'm fine..." You say, now a little unsure.

He looks up, squinting. "Must be the sun. You know, with climate change and sunspots and the hole in the ozone. Cosmic rays. Scrambling our brains."

Now that he mentions it, you do feel a little weird. But he looks OK. You ask him if he's feeling anything.

"Oh, yeah. I almost passed out a few hours ago. I've been laying down inside and just came outside. I'm going to stay under this awning."

"But I have to walk to work," you say, looking up fearfully, "and it's another six blocks."

"Hmmm," he says, scratching his chin. "It would be best if you could stay under the awning with me, or go inside, but..." He snaps his fingers. "I've got an idea!"

"Yeah?" you ask hopefully, almost desperately. "What should I do?"

"Well, I've got this truckload of sombreros. Brims as big as this awning…"

The power of narrative can work both ways: for you, or on you. Be wise, do good, and live free.

• • •

- 77 -

Most of what is wise and good isn't complicated, just hard.

Doing the right thing is not always easy. No one ever said it would be. But the biggest part of doing the right thing is doing it, regardless of how difficult it might be. But when we label a situation as "complicated," we convince ourselves that the right thing in that situation is somehow unknowable, so unclear that we cannot be held accountable for neglecting it or quitting.

There are some complicated things in life, even some that are very complicated, but not as many as we like to think. We like to point out the difficult cases and the terrible dilemmas. But those are usually the exceptions, not the rule. The truth is, we often use "complicated" as an excuse to avoid clear, hard truths. We don't want to admit that we know what the right thing to do is, and we don't want to do it.

Wisdom and goodness are often hard, but usually not complicated. Dunking a basketball is not complicated; it's just hard. Running a marathon is not complicated, just hard. Keeping our promises is usually not complicated, but it can often be hard. Sometimes, keeping our wedding vows is complicated, but most of the time it's just hard. Being responsible with our money, maintaining our bodies, loving our neighbor, honoring our parents, being loyal to our friends and country, providing for our children, etc.—all of these are rarely complicated. They are often just hard work. Wisdom and goodness and freedom are not free. They require courage, discipline, and faithfulness. We often pay for them by giving up our time, pride, and pleasures. We must put a lot of sweat equity into virtue.

• • •

- 78 -

Why are you getting life advice from songs and movies? Have you ever met the people who write songs and movies? If you did, you wouldn't take their advice on anything.

Pop music and movies entertain and inspire us, but they also fill our minds with powerful images and ideas. Those images and ideas put down roots in our imagination, which then bear fruit. And we pluck and eat it.

We think we know about love and life, but too many of our opinions are the unexamined harvest of a lifetime of popular culture. Decades of listening and watching have shaped our internal landscape. We don't understand why we feel the way we do, and it really doesn't bother us that we don't know. While the primary influences on earlier generations might have been the Bible, teachers, or elders, our wise men are song and screenwriters.

And that is a problem.

If you were to sit across from one of them in a coffee shop and listen to them describe their lives, you would probably snicker or gape in disbelief because most of these people cannot maintain a relationship, hold a job, or even keep their plants alive. You wouldn't hire them if you owned a business, you wouldn't trust them with your children, and you certainly wouldn't turn to them for counseling.

But put their opinions into a film with a good soundtrack, or have them croon it under a spotlight with a room of screaming, swooning fans, and it seems to us like the wisdom of the ages.

Here's a better idea. When you are faced with a choice, get advice from someone who has proven success solving that problem. If you're looking for advice on love and marriage, don't get it from a singer-songwriter with twenty-seven failed relationships; talk to someone who's been happily married for fifty or sixty years. Whatever they tell you, do that. If you are trying to find your career path, don't make decisions based on a movie you saw. The screenwriter has never held a job for more than nine months. Talk to someone who just retired from a successful career.

The wise, good, and free person seeks the wealth of the generations, the accumulated experience of those who have lived shrewdly, decently, and maintained their liberty from all the snares of foolishness and evil.

• • •

- 79 -

Whenever my kids say, "But didn't you do that when you were young?" My answer is always, "Don't be like me. Be *better* than me."

Hypocrisy is a serious charge. Jesus didn't like hypocrites, and none of us do either. Which is why our kids delight in discovering that we once tasted the fruit we have forbidden them. They think they have just kicked our feet out from underneath us, and we have no leg to stand on by denying them the folly of our youth. I told my dad that I could be as bad as he was, and I've heard my kids toss my youthful indiscretions back in my face.

But I don't want my kids to be as dumb as I was. I don't want the apple to fall close to the tree. I not only want them to have more than I did, I want them to be better than I was. More than that, I want them to be better than I am or will ever be. I want them to be so wise, good, and free that I can go to them for advice and help and inspiration.

But that requires humility—genuine humility, not false modesty and insincere regret. That sort of humility arises from repentance, true sorrow for the wrong we have done and the good we have left undone. And that only comes from awareness of the gap between your actual qualities and what is truly wise, good and free.

Instinct drives us to reproduce ourselves, to create new versions of us. We must not pass on our failures and family curses.

But if we really do love our children, then we want them to be wiser, better, and more free than we ever were—and for them to teach us a thing or two someday.

• • •

- 80 -

Guilt is good. If you did a bad thing, then you should feel guilty. That's called conscience. Losing it has not produced a better world.

Guilt is a critical self-defense mechanism. It is the moral equivalent of pain. Just as pain warns us that the stove is hot and that we'd better stop touching it, guilt monitors our ethical behavior and tells us when to pull back before we or someone else gets hurt. Depending on the action, wrongdoing might most obviously hurt someone else. But sin (and I don't mind calling it that) diminishes us, as well. It corrodes our heart, weakens our mind, limits our potential, dulls our senses, and enslaves our future.

We might argue about the moral laws, about which actions are sins. But I've never met anyone who genuinely believes there is no such thing as right and wrong; even atheists and relativists have their ethical codes (about which they are often as rigid and judgmental as any Puritan). Our feel-good culture's conviction that guilt is bad is unsustainable and self-destructive.

If I've heard it once, I've heard it a thousand times: we're not supposed to make people feel guilty. And I basically agree with that. We shouldn't "make people feel guilty," if by that we mean that we shouldn't manufacture or manipulate guilt in other people, especially for our own purposes. But if we facilitate a guilty person becoming aware of and confronting the wrong they have done (or are still doing), aren't we helping them? Shouldn't we help people to become wise, good, and free? Their guilt isn't holding them back, but the things they are doing, for which they are guilty of, are. Wisdom, goodness, and freedom will only come when they discover, own their errors, repent, and change.

But guilt without the possibility of grace is shame. And that is another subject, and there is a Story for that.

• • •

- 81 -

Satire is easy. So is criticism. Being constructive and productive—building something worthwhile—is hard. Making something look stupid afterwards is easy. Critics can always look smart by cracking jokes.

I love a good joke. Most of the time this means that I laugh when a witty critic finds the funny flaws in a person, place, or thing. Satire is an art form, criticism served up with just enough humor to keep it from feeling mean spirited.

But in the field of human endeavor, cracking jokes is easy compared to creating something of value. Satire can be brilliant, but it's a deconstructive brilliance. The person who tears things down for a living depends on those who build, but builders don't need critics whose only purpose is to cynically point out their mistakes. Criticism, and fear of it, can force the builder to see things he missed, or drive him to create something better able to withstand the withering scrutiny. But the mocker contributes no substance and adds no value to the project.

We need to be careful that we don't mistake this sort of clever, caustic humor for actual intelligence, much less wisdom. The comedian in the satirical TV sketch might seem shrewd and well informed. But he looks worldly and wise because he only has to sit on the sideline and shoot at the man in the arena who had the initiative and talent to create something that drew a crowd. The comedian just works the crowd for jokes. The worst thing we can do is to make the comedian and critic our leader, or look to him as our wise man.

• • •

- 82 -

We can blather on about there being no objective truth, but no one can actually live that way. Do you want to drive over a bridge designed by someone who thinks that there is no such thing as a right or wrong answer?

• • •

- 83 -

John Adams pointed out that facts are stubborn things. Experience ought to also teach us that math is merciless and physics is a bitch. If you are expecting the universe to give your half-baked plans a break, refigure your calculations. Believe in miracles, but don't count on them.

We have a remarkable capacity to ignore the hard data of life. Even scientists cherry pick data to support their worldview. We all know (or should) that statistics become squishy in the service of agendas. Two and two always equals four, but far too often we pretend it doesn't when we're budgeting and spending—whether it is for our family, our business, or our nation. And we hopefully invest in any number of gadgets and "emerging technologies" that are as plausible as perpetual motion or alchemy (turning lead into gold).

The hard facts of the universe are part of the landscape over which the game of life is played. The goalposts do not move. You do not have superpowers: step off a cliff and you fall to your death. You cannot draw a square circle, and financial equations do not care about your hopes and dreams.

This is what makes miracles so rare and wonderful. Every now and then God intervenes, adjusts the facts, and suspends the laws. You can pray for a miracle, and you can even have faith that you will get one. But they are called miracles because they are rare, and God grants them on his timetable and for his purposes.

Willful ignorance of reality and a generally hopeful attitude are not much of a plan and are rarely winning strategies. They are more likely to get you hurt. Badly. You can never see around the corners or ahead to the next page of your story. But in general, check and recheck your facts, knots, and math.

• • •

- 84 -

A marriage is a lot of things, but one of them is a small business. When we wed, we start a for-profit corporation. We buy and own property, and we acquire wealth that we hope to pass on to our children (or a charity). This is one reason why marriage is hard work. It's also one of the many reasons to marry wisely: in addition to everything else, you are choosing a business partner.

From time immemorial, everyone understood that marriage was a merger-acquisition, a for-profit venture in which a new legal entity was formed. That was the idea behind dowries, name changes, rings, and all the rest. The old wedding vows made this explicit, with some phrase like, "With my body and property, I thee wed." This didn't exclude love, by any means. But the family has always been (and should always remain) the basic unit of society. Our work and wealth are not due to the state, but to our spouse and children. That's one reason the Bible says that a man shall leave his parents and become one flesh with his wife: society grows and expands by two individuals forming a new, corporate unit and depending on that unit to provide for them.

In our society, three things are undermining the family as a small business. First, we have made marriage about feelings and self-fulfillment only, to the exclusion of the practical structure it provides (it should be both). Second, divorce, sexual relationships, and intentional childbearing outside marriage have weakened confidence in the "institution of marriage" (the term is now a source of derision). Business success requires confidence in market, and there is too little for many couples to invest in their future together. Third, we increasingly look to the state as the basic unit of society, with people depending on it, rather than their family, for their future. That is why collectivist and totalitarian (forgive the redundancy) governments always try to undermine marriage and family bonds. The family is a threat to the state.

• • •

- 85 -

When imagination and vision run too far ahead of ability and execution, nothing gets done and the enterprise is eventually going to stall out.

• • •

- 86 -

Anger is easy. Love is an uphill effort, against the gravity of our nature. But anger runs downhill, gaining momentum as it is drawn into the gravity well of our broken humanity. Anger consumes your mind, corrupts your soul, and constricts your actions. When anger rules your life, you cannot be wise, good, or free.

Of course there is a time when anger is appropriate. In the Bible, we read that even Jesus got angry at times. But we also read that at times he wept as well. But neither characterized his life. Emotions like anger and grief are useful responses to particular situations. They channel our reactions, sometimes into useful actions.

But anger is one of the most, if not the most, corrosive substances in the universe. The angry young man becomes the mean old man. The angry girl becomes the bitter old woman. The occasional righteous reaction to injustice has its place in life, but anger can quickly become a runaway train, rolling downhill and becoming the dominant theme in a life. Angry people start out being angry about some injustice, then become angry about injustice in the world in general, then start looking for some injustice to stay angry about. Like a virus, anger is always seeking a new host.

An angry life can never be a wise, good, or free life. Because anger clouds judgment, wisdom is impossible. Because anger rots your soul and leaves no room in your heart for loving another person (other than some fanciful love of intangible concepts like humanity, patriotism, or justice), it is impossible to be good. And because anger takes over your life and limits your choices, it makes freedom an impossibility. Let it go.

• • •

- 87 -

Buying yourself time buys you possibility. The worst-case scenario is probably not inevitable. Stay calm, keep your eyes open, and keep your head on a swivel. Prepare yourself to take advantage of opportunities. People who follow this strategy are often called "lucky."

There is a story about an ancient con man that served a king as the court magician. For some reason, he fell out of favor with the monarch. The king ordered his head to be chopped off, and the guards stepped forward to frog-march him from the throne room. As they grabbed him, he called out, "Wait, your highness! What if I could teach your cat to sing and dance?"

The king raised his hand and the guards stopped. "Could you really do such a thing?"

"Absolutely," said the magician. "And with a dancing, singing cat, you would become the richest, most famous king in the whole world!"

"This is true," said the king, daydreaming while petting the cat on his lap. "How long would it take?"

"One year," said the magician.

"Very well!" the King pronounced. "I will give you one year, locked in the tower with Fluffy. If on this day, twelve months from now, Fluffy cannot entertain the court, then your head will be on a stick outside the walls as a warning to others not to lie to me."

Fluffy was handed to the magician, and they were marched to the tower. As they climbed the stairs, one of the guards, who was friendly to the magician, asked him if he was crazy. "Do you really think you can pull this off?"

"Probably not," shrugged the magician. "But a lot can happen in a year. The king might die. The cat might die. I might die—or escape. And who knows, the cat just might learn to sing and dance. We'll have to see what happens."

• • •

- 88 -

Most of what promises to be "life changing" isn't. It might *affect* your life, but it takes a lot to really change it. Personally, I'd be cautious about anything that promises to change my life. Change it *how*?

• • •

- 89 -

Just because you are qualified for a job doesn't mean that you'll get it. Being qualified only gets you seriously considered, because everyone who is seriously considered is qualified. Your story is what makes you unique.

Being qualified is not enough.

Lots of people go through life thinking that it is. They're certain that because they have the right degree, certificate, or required experience that they have what it takes to get a job. But qualifications only get you considered; they don't get you chosen unless there is no one else who's qualified.

Be honest: is it enough to make you want to be friends with someone? Because they're "qualified" to be your friend? To work or collaborate with someone on a project? Do you fall in love with someone because they're "qualified?" Do you choose products or services or restaurants because they're "good enough?"

To put it into philosophical terms, your skills are a necessary but not sufficient in order to compete in the marketplace.

The reality is that you have to market yourself, especially in a competitive job marketplace. It's rarely a simple contest of qualifications. For highly prized positions, everyone who applies is qualified. What sets you apart? It isn't just that you're more qualified. You can't just win it on some points scale. You have to connect with your customer, which in the job market is the person who makes the hiring decisions.

Your goal should be to let someone know who you are, beyond just what you've done. Once you're in the door somewhere, no one cares about your résumé anymore. It's what kind of person that you are and what you bring to the organization that matters. Most people who are doing the hiring realize this. They're looking for someone that they want to have around.

• • •

- 90 -

Managing life is mostly managing conflict. From Cain and Abel to the coworker at the next desk, from the neighbor next door or the spouse next to you in bed, life is a dance with people who hear their own tune and keep stepping on your feet. How you solve that problem determines how successful you can be.

Conflict seems like an unnecessary distraction. It's frustrating enough that someone is bumping into us, but we get irritated that we have to deal with this intrusion into all the really important stuff we have to deal with. But conflict is the core of the human experience; there will be friction as any collection of individuals tries to live and work in community. It is not a distraction from the important things in life, it is the important thing. You will never accomplish anything of significance in life without managing conflict along the way. If you manage it badly, you might still be able to point to some big things that you got done, but I guarantee you that they came at tremendous cost to you and/or others. And I also predict that, as great as those accomplishments might be, your life as a whole will be no more successful than your ability to manage and solve the conflicts with the people around you. Don't believe me? Read some historical biographies. None of the great men and women of history did it alone, and their achievements have so often been overshadowed or even undone by the broken relationships they left in their wake.

Let's be clear: this isn't just about your personal life. Conflict management is just as important with coworkers and customers as it is with friends and family. It doesn't matter how smart you are or how hard you work. If you run the race of your career by swerving and banging into the other cars, the best you can hope for is to roll across the finish line a dented mess with a lot of angry people behind you. Is that winning?

• • •

- 91 -

Of course there is a Military-Industrial Complex, and it has an effect in American political culture. But there is also an Academia-Media Complex, a Financial Industry-Treasury Department Complex, and the Government-Public Employee Unions Complex. And the biggest complex of all: the I'm-Entitled-To-Get-Free-Stuff-From-the-Government Complex.

• • •

- 92 -

A lot of success comes from just marching on. Every day, get up and move forward. Somehow. You will be surprised by what you can accomplish over time. Unless you're going in the wrong direction, in which case you are trudging deeper into failure. Regularly check your navigation.

There are not many sure things in life, but this is one of them: if you stop moving, you stop getting closer to your destination. The clock never stops, and whenever you do, time is running out to get whatever matters to you done. While you sit, wherever you are going gets no closer. If it's a moving target, it might be getting further away.

There are a lot of variables that contribute to success, but a few constants as well. Here's one of them: achievement is incremental and cumulative. I suppose that at some time, somewhere, someone was brilliant or lucky enough to become an overnight success, but I can't think of any names off the top of my head. Most overnight successes are the fruit of many years of hard work finally coming together or being recognized. Most of what we call luck is the intersection of preparation and opportunity. It does no good to be in the right place in the right time if you are the wrong person to take advantage of it.

But trudging resolutely in the wrong direction—ignoring all signs, advice, and lack of results—is a special kind of foolishness.

It takes stupid pride in its commitment to continue despite any indication of progress.

The bold sailors in the Age of Navigation covered vast oceans at the pace of a leisurely walk. But they constantly checked their navigation. Regularly consult the wisdom of past generations, seek advice from others that are wise, good, and free, and plot your progress against known landmarks.

• • •

- 93 -

You probably can't change your life in a week, but you could in a year. Over a decade, you could change a lot of other people's lives. Over your lifetime, you might be able to set into motion forces that change the world. But you have to do it in that order.

I'm constantly amazed by how many experiences or products claim to be life changing. Setting aside my concern that not all change is for the better, it is rarely rapid. The law of inertia tells us that objects at rest stay at rest, and objects in motion stay in motion, unless an outside force is used to change their state. The more mass the object has, the more energy it takes to change its state of inertia. Human lives have a lot of mass, and thus a lot of inertia. They don't change quickly, easily, or cheaply. It takes a lot of time and energy to change a life. And when a lot of lives are cobbled together in a family, community, or organization, the inertia is cumulative. Changing a family is a lot harder than changing a member of that family. Changing the civilization and values of a planet is a daunting proposition.

But while we grossly overestimate what we could do in the short term, we grossly underestimate what we can do over time with a really big idea and enough energy behind it. Real change comes from ideas that change people by making themselves see their place in the universe in a different way, and keeps keep them moving toward something they want to be more than what they are.

But you cannot take humanity, or even a small part of it, somewhere you have not been yourself. Do you want to change the world? Begin by changing yourself, today. Be patient and persistent, and move toward wisdom, goodness, and freedom. Over time, you might help shift a planet.

• • •

- 94 -

We need the right amount of organization in our lives. Too little and things fall into chaos. Too much, and our lives have no substance in the center: we spend our time alphabetizing the soup cans in the cupboard.

• • •

- 95 -

It seems silly to even have to point this out, but be prepared to die.
At any moment.

The reasons many clichés became clichés in the first place is because they are true, and everyone knows it.

Do we really need to be reminded of how fragile life is? How at any minute all sorts of bad things could snuff our wicks? We all know this intellectually, and it fills some of us with constant anxiety. I've never met anyone who didn't admit that they should live every day prepared for it to be their last, but I've met few who actually were.

This is all so obvious to everyone, but so is *eat less and exercise more,* and we don't do that either. Are your finances and affairs in order if someone T-bones your car in an intersection today? I know it's morbid to think about. But to tell you the truth, mine are not, even as I write this advice. I'm too busy, and it's too unpleasant to think about, much less do.

What about your family? I've been around a number of dying people. Do you know what people mostly talk about when they are dying? Their family. For some, it's recalling the joys. Others regret the failures and fractures and would give anything at that moment to go back and do things differently. Start doing things differently, right now. Put the book down, and reconcile with those you love.

What about your faith? That's the other thing people talk about when they are dying. When the plane lurches and starts to fall from the sky, everyone prays to God and pleads to see their family one more time. Make peace with both God and family before it's too late. That's how you live a life that is wise, good, and free.

• • •

- 96 -

When traveling, have as little impact on those around you as possible. Being contained in small spaces for long periods with strangers is hard enough without you making it worse.

I love to travel—not only the getting there, but the going as well. It's exciting to get into the car, onto the train, or hear the call to board at an airport gate. It feels like an adventure is about to start.

Travel has its challenges, of course, not the least of which is being confined with other people along the way. John Paul Satre said, "Hell is other people." As a general rule, I ignore everything Satre said, but when it comes to traveling companions, he makes a good point. So, please do not be "that guy" (or "that lady"). Do not:

- Spread yourself over the armrest into my space.
- Pass gas into recirculating air at 30,000 feet.
- Change the radio or CD without asking when it's my turn to drive.

- Be obnoxious, loud, and demanding when I am trapped eighteen inches from you.
- Do anything creepy or weird in a room that I have to share with you.

Aside from pleading with you to not ruin my journey if I'm stuck alongside you, here's my larger point: be considerate of other people under stressful circumstances. A wise, good, and free person is also street smart. He or she has worldly experience, and can function well in society. And in the globalized 21st century, few of us live anymore in isolated villages within a ten-mile radius of where we were born. That means we need to be able to travel well, getting along with others en route and when we get there.

Be a good companion, a considerate seatmate, and a kind fellow passenger. Think about how your actions affect those around you, even if they are total strangers who speak another language. Cultivate patience, adaptability, and good manners. Through kindness and self-control, let's prove that Satre didn't know what he was talking about.

• • •

- 97 -

Do not confuse heroism and celebrity. Some of the greatest heroes are unknown and unsung. Many famous people are not admirable.

• • •

- 98 -

Don't panic. Ever. There is no scenario in which panicking helps.

The ability to think clearly and act decisively is probably the most important factor in surviving a crisis. Intelligence, education (in relevant subjects), strength, and skills are all important tools, but self-control and calm judgment allow you to pick and use those tools as needed. Panic is a disease, a loss of humanity that makes us worse than beasts. Animals at least have some hard-wired instincts that kick in during a survival situation. Modern humans are reduced to infants, and infants are helpless.

You can't predict who will maintain self-mastery and calm during a crisis. It's not obvious by looking at people. The accomplished, tough-talking executive might freak out and do one dumb thing after another, while the quiet teenage girl might keep her head and make it through. Training helps (that's the point of the endless rehearsals for disaster in the military, emergency services, and airlines). But training cannot put in what God left out: in the end, panic or self-control are character issues. As the cliché goes, crisis doesn't create character; it reveals it.

Setting aside tsunamis, plane crashes, and bear attacks, I see a lot of slow motion panic in slow motion emergencies. I see people who have lost jobs or have failing businesses lose their ability to think clearly while acting calmly and decisively. It might take place over a year instead of five minutes, but the response is the same: they lose the ability to control their thoughts, emotions, and actions. Whether it is a bad diagnosis, a bad economy, or a bad marriage, nothing gets better because you panic. It is the opposite of wisdom, goodness, and freedom.

• • •

- 99 -

None of us wants to be petty. But one person's pettiness is another person's principle. It's hard to know which hills to die on. Pick yours carefully.

No one who bickers over small matters believes that they are small. They matter to them.

You cannot and should not concede your principles because someone thinks they are no big deal. But there are three things that you can and should do before you try and hold some point of ground like the Spartans at Thermopylae.

First, consider why the other party doesn't find this issue to be a matter of principle. I'm not saying that you will change your mind, but it's at least possible that you might be making a bigger deal out of this thing than you should.

Second, even if it is a principle, is it worth the cost to defend it? I believe in martyrdom for a worthy cause, but not all causes are worth losing your family, friends, fortune, or life. Is it worth breaking community, churches, corporations, or countries over? Some things are, absolutely. But some are not.

Third, even if it is a principle worth defending, is there another way to do it? Can you convince the other person instead of fighting them? Can you win them over time with love instead of running over them with arguments or force? Can you accomplish more by engaging them instead of pulling back?

• • •

- 100 -

There is an art to picking what to worry about. Concern, skepticism, and even fear are necessary tools for surviving a dangerous world. The trick—often the line between success and failure—is to be the right amount of worried about the right things. But going through life anxious, assuming the worst about people, and obsessing about the wrong things, is the opposite of being wise, good, and free.

I have friend who owns a business in a turbulent industry. In recent years, the economy has left his company battered and bruised—but still standing. But many of his competitors didn't survive at all. A while back, I was having a drink with him and asked him how he has managed to stay alive on a field where so many others have fallen.

He looked at his pint a bit before he spoke. "Everyone around me—my wife, kids, employees, friends—says I'm too uptight and cynical and pessimistic." Then he looked up and blurted out, "But I think I'm just the right amount of uptight and cynical and pessimistic. My company survives on my finely tuned neuroses/pathology. I am so worried about making payroll that I overcompensate and do whatever I need to do to keep our sales pipeline full."

By contrast, I know someone whom no contractor ever works for a second time. He operates on the assumption that everyone is incompetent and a cheat. He worries that the waitress will get his order wrong, that the cook will screw up his steak, that the cashier will overcharge his card. He can't drop his clothes off at a dry cleaner, convinced that his buttons will get chipped up. He can't hire a gardener, because the grass might get cut wrong.

Wisdom calibrates our concerns, so we can be good to others and ourselves living free to enjoy what life actually offers, not what we insist upon.

• • •

- 101 -

Technology makes it too easy to react quickly without thinking things through. Sit on that email, text, or online posting for a day. Maybe two. Are you *sure* that you want to send it?

Our thoughts and emotions are volatile. That's not new, nor is our tendency to blurt out something we regret later. But the technological advances of the last couple of generations have given global reach and the pixelated permanence of poorly considered stupid rants and shared feelings.

I love to write pointed emails to vent my outrage or clever online posts that share more of my thoughts than is prudent. It feels so good to unleash the pixels like little soldiers for my cause.

It's also unwise, often not good, and shackles me to consequences from which I would rather be free.

I've had confrontations that required a follow up meeting in a distant city. As I got on an airplane or started driving, I imagined all sorts of clever comebacks and nasty retorts I could unleash when I got there. But the hours and miles melted my indignation or demands. By the time I got to the meeting, wisdom had tempered my temper or moderated my agenda. The delay prevented a conflict from becoming a train wreck. In many cases it helped me find a way to reverse a bad situation.

Just because you have the technology to communicate at near the speed of light doesn't mean that you have to. Slow down, and be wise. Let good come out of your mouth or keyboard. Don't let hasty reactions drop anchors that limit your freedom.

• • •

- 102 -

Why do acts of love and devotion make the hairs on our neck stand up? They make no sense as evolutionary behaviors. I think that we are glimpsing something holy, and our reflexes remind us that we were made for more than we can see in this world.

• • •

- 103 -

Quitting isn't always a failure. It might be a sign of intelligence, or even integrity. Sometimes, when you know you're not the right person for the job or this isn't the right job for you, the best thing you can do for everyone involved is to just walk away.

Some people discover that they are a round peg stuck into a square hole. As with so many things in life, self-awareness is the beginning of wisdom. But what to do about it?

It depends on what the hole is, and how you got into it. If it's your marriage, then you adapt, because you gave a sacred vow, for life, to do so. If it's the military, you signed the papers and took an oath, and need to do your duty and see it through. If it's a child you created or adopted, it's time to grow up and be responsible.

But if you've taken a job or started a business, and come to realize that it's a bad fit, digging in might not be a good long-term strategy. Of course a job is work, and being a grown up is doing the work you are given without complaining to support yourself and your family. But if you are not good at your job and realize that you never will be, who is benefitting from you being a bad employee or incompetent business owner? Organizations are full of mediocre workers who somehow find a niche and can't be dislodged (especially in union-protected industries). Business owners might find a way to stumble along, barely making it. But it's not good for anyone (including the family you support) if you spend decades as a round peg in a square hole, never discovering your potential or tasting success.

I'm not necessarily telling you to quit your job if it's the wrong job for you. But I am telling you to consider it. Get some advice from someone who is wise, good, and free who can help you to become the same.

• • •

- 104 -

Optimism and energy are not functions of age. Largely, they are habits of mind. Grumpy and tired old people have probably always been that way. Optimistic young people who can't sit still keep going until they can't. Be careful about who you are, because that is who you are becoming.

Character doesn't change much over time. I've heard various estimates about how the age that a person's character is largely set. But I think it's fair to say that by the time we are ten years old our character and personality have assumed their default shape. Of course the events of life impact us, but rarely do they make us into a completely different kind of person. Changing a person's basic character and personality takes an enormous amount of effort.

This is why our assumptions that young people are energetic optimists and old people are tired old codgers are off base. Yes, we have less physical energy when we get older. But there is a difference between having less physical energy and being lazy. Lots of lazy young people have plenty of energy to burn. Lots of old people are constantly working, thinking, and producing, even though they get out of breath sometimes. Energy is a physical trait but laziness is a character flaw.

Optimism is the same way. Lots of young people, with many years and opportunities ahead of them, are pessimistic and grumpy. Lots of old people, with a limited number of years and options, wake up every day convinced that some good could happen. Optimism is a character asset.

Whatever your character and personality type, you tend to become more of as you get older. Which is why we should be very careful about who we are. If we want to live wise, good, and free throughout our life, we start now. If we are not, we never will be.

• • •

- 105 -

You are responsible for your actions, not for another person's reactions.

You can't control how other people think, feel, or behave. Despite your best efforts, they sometimes respond to what you say or do in disappointing or even disastrous ways. Often, we feel responsible for these outcomes. We wish that we could control them, and sometimes we feel guilty that we can't. But other people are other people. They have their own hearts and minds and make their own choices. You are not the author of their stories.

You do have control over what you think and feel, say and do. You may argue that you aren't completely responsible for all of your inner and outer life, but if not you, then who? The burden of proof is on you to show why you aren't, not on those who want to hold you accountable.

Have you been fair, kind, wise, honest, and gracious in what you have thought about other people? What you have said and done to them or about them? If so, then they are accountable if they reacted unfairly, unkindly, foolishly, dishonestly, and ungraciously to you. You've done all that you can.

This is both good and bad news. You don't have to feel guilty if you did the right thing and they did the wrong. On the other hand, are you sure that you have done the right thing? And don't congratulate yourself for great relationships if you've behaved badly toward them and they were more generous toward you than you deserved.

Personal responsibility is the pivot on which people turn, either toward wisdom, goodness, and freedom, or toward foolishness, evil, and slavery.

• • •

- 106 -

People, especially students, often ask, "What does God want me to do with my life?" Near as I can tell, hardly anyone is ever told that. But if we listen, God will tell us what to do *next*.

• • •

- 107 -

People without curiosity often wonder why they did not get ahead. Without intellectual curiosity, you learn nothing, change little, and never discover what's over the next hill.

Curiosity is an essential element of wisdom, goodness, and freedom.

Without wisdom, your thinking is either magical (you just hope things turn out well) or mechanical (you live by rules and routine). To become wise, you must learn not only what is true and what works, but why and how. That allows you to react to change, adapt over time, and teach others. And that kind of knowledge is the result of curiosity about the world, and life in it.

Goodness and freedom are not just qualities, they are choices. To be truly good and free, we need to know what evil and enslavement look like, and avoid them. We don't need to learn by experience. In the story of Adam and Eve, Satan lies when he tells them that they can only become wise by tasting the fruit of the Tree of the Knowledge of Good and Evil. For them to become wise, good and free, they needed a choice. They chose foolishness, sin, and enslavement. It wasn't too much curiosity that led them to listen to the snake, it was too little. They should have asked more questions before they acted.

Never treat learning as a chore or discovery as a burden. Without curiosity, you will stay exactly as you are.

• • •

- 108 -

There are plenty of good ideas for businesses. What's rare is the ability to bring an idea into reality and to grow it into a profitable and sustainable enterprise. A wise, good, and free government would make that as easy as possible.

I hear good business ideas on a regular basis. (Unfortunately, I hear bad business ideas far more often, perhaps on a 5:1 ratio.) There is no shortage of great ideas or talented, hardworking people to launch them.

The hard part is thousands of tiny choices that must be made along the way from idea to enterprise. Luck is not as big of a factor as some believe. Of course some discover gold on their property or have a tornado wipe out their crop. But the shrewd and talented business owner prepares for opportunities and disasters and makes good decisions on the fly as they occur.

Some people have a gift for making shrewd business decisions. They are wise, valuable, and independent, and they stay that way through the inevitable ups and downs of starting and sustaining a business.

Some people have reverse alchemy: they turn gold into lead. If that's you—if you tend to make foolish decisions, behave badly, and are constantly enslaving yourself to debt, bad relationships, and addictions—you should probably not start a business, no matter how brilliant your idea is.

Government should not make gifted entrepreneurs paddle upstream, while enabling dysfunctional business owners by insuring them from the consequences of their bad decisions. That is a tide that will lower all boats.

• • •

- 109 -

Think bigger, but act smaller.

Some people are big picture visionaries, and some are detail oriented. Some can see the forest through the trees, and some fly so far above the forest they can't see the individual trees. Don't be either of those types.

If our minds are full of little thoughts, little hurts, little ambitions, and little rivalries, we become little people. Think big: see the big picture, get plugged into the bigger world around you, follow the big ideas, cast big visions and pursue big goals. Expand the quantity and quality of your professional network.

But big thinking can lead to big problems: grandiosity, arrogance, and elitism. Don't become so enamored with the forest that you can't see the trees; much less accomplish anything of practical value. Think big, at the 30,000 foot strategy level, but act practically and get things done on the ground. Dreamers and idealists are great, but be the dreamer that can do and the idealist that can implement.

Don't just dream, do. You will become immensely valuable to everyone around you.

• • •

- 110 -

Every business has a thousand critics who think they know how it works, or how it should work. But unless someone grasps the money part—how it's made and where it goes—they will never understand that business or be able to offer an intelligent critique.

Follow the money.

Businesses exist to make it. No one starts a lemonade stand, or lasts long selling lemonade, unless they know where the money comes from, how much of it there is, and where it goes. Everyone around the lemonade stand, even the other kids the owner hires to help him, will have an opinion about how it could be better. But at its core, everything revolves around revenue and returns. Money is blood in the veins of a business. It's positive and negative qualities can usually be explained, and predicted, by the flow of its cash.

I have heard employees pound their chest and say that the owners don't understand the business because they don't know what it's like to perform some function on the shop floor. But that employee and the job he does are like part of the body. The money that flows to and from that part is what explains why and how and how long that part will function within the body. The CEO may not know how to do your job, but if you don't follow the money you will never understand his.

To be blunt: bosses or owners who don't grasp the money part of the business won't be bosses or owners for long.

Customers can and will take their business elsewhere. But when they can't understand why the business won't respond to their needs and wants, the answer almost always has to do with where the money comes from and goes.

To succeed in business, you must master the money part. An owner must always know where it is coming from, how much of it there is, and where it is going.

• • •

- 111 -

Negative, inflexible, and passive: three qualities that will make you the least likely to survive in a crisis.

We've all read books or seen movies about a random group of strangers, stranded together by some crisis (shipwreck, plane crash, earthquake, war, alien invasion, etc.). Any storyteller worth her salt will introduce the characters carefully, with some intentional misdirection. The big, strong guy looks like he will do just fine, while the mousy, little lady will probably fall apart at the first sign of trouble. In the second act of the story, you will be surprised as the strong man's character flaws and errors of judgment doom him to a quick end, while the little lady rises to the occasion.

In real life, there are a thousand variables to who survives in a crisis. Where you sat on the plane, which floor of the building you worked on, or which immunities your DNA carried are unknowable and uncontrollable. And the factors that contribute to survival could fill a book.

But three factors that will dramatically lower your chance of surviving any crisis (physical, financial, family, etc.) are: a negative attitude, inflexible thinking, and a passive personality. If you have all three, you are the least likely to emerge from whatever crucible you are going through unscathed.

By contrast, an optimistic attitude allows you to endure hardship. Flexible thinking allows you to adapt your behavior. And proactive personalities make their own luck, by preparing for and seizing any opportunities that present themselves.

Life is full of all sorts of traumatic situations. Prepare yourself by changing yourself before they hit.

• • •

- 112 -

There's a time to look and listen, a time to think, and a time to be still, ponder, and let your decision grow to fruition. After all that, it's time to act. Make sure you do it in that order. Jumbling it up causes all sorts of problems.

The evaluate-think-decide-act loop is a critical life skill. It is not instinctive or intuitive, at least in humans. Sometimes we listen, sometimes we think, sometimes we ponder, and sometimes we act—but not in a consistent pattern.

The good news is that this pattern can be taught and learned. Pilots, for example, are so well trained in a similar decision-making loop that it becomes instinctive for them. We ought to be training our children, very early on, to do the same thing.

Every step in that loop has great value. Some of us tend to favor one over the other, by preference, personality, or habit. Some of us take in endless information, which is great, if we do something with it. Some of us like to think things over, but without curiosity and investigation we have too many variables to solve the problem. Some of us like to contemplate our decisions, but that's not the same as thinking them through and analyzing the information. And some of us are all about the action, which is the point of the process. But if we act first, we are just reacting mindlessly.

I've called it a loop, because as soon as we act, we move back around and start looking and listening again. What has changed after we made our move? What does our next move need to be?

Do you want to be wise, good, and free? Then practice this loop, in everything you do. Master it, and you will master yourself.

• • •

- 113 -

Unspoken conflict festers like an infection below the surface. Lance it, drain the pus, and let air cleanse the wound. Don't let it rot and poison the relationship, or even your heart. If it's in your home, don't let it ruin your family's life.

• • •

- 114 -

Inspiration is for amateurs. Pros do the work.

Creative professionals can create on demand. They don't need inspiration; they have mastered their craft and know how to cultivate ideas when they need them. More than that, they know how to take whatever ideas are available and develop them into finished products to meet demands and deadlines. Of course some ideas are better than others, and not all projects turn out equally well. But over time, professional creatives can deliver consistent work. Amateurs who wait around for the muse to strike and do nothing unless they feel like it are not serious. They get left behind.

Do you want to create? Learn your craft, and learn to work hard.

• • •

- 115 -

Of course religious people will vote their conscience, and act out of their convictions. What would be disturbing is if they didn't.

• • •

- 116 -

Anarchy is not the absence of government. In practice, anarchy is rule by the strong, the violent, and the ruthless. Most of the social malcontents and trendy intellectuals who talk glibly about anarchy would be the first ones eaten alive if it ever came.

By contrast, civilization is a hard-earned infrastructure that preserves life, liberty, and the pursuit of happiness for the weak and defenseless. It's not yet perfected, and its path has been bumpy. But the blessings of civilization have been purchased in blood. We must work hard to improve it, but never disrespect it. Guard it with vigilance, or the dark and stupid and violent monsters that lie just beyond the walls will sack the city.

• • •

- 117 -

Markets are a *descriptive* concept: they tell us what people actually want, and will do. Socialism is *prescriptive* concept: it tells people what they should want, and have to do. In the end, socialism never works, for a variety of reasons, but among them is that you can never make people buy things they don't want for very long.

• • •

- 118 -
Give a jackass a microphone, and all you get is a loud jackass.

In our media-driven culture, we confuse visibility and celebrity with quality and credibility. It is easy to fall into the error of believing that the media world is the real world: that what happens online and on TV is what really matters. If you say ridiculous or offensive things to a few people, and you're an annoying crank. If you can reach a million people, you become a voice that deserves to be heard, and your lousy book, song, movie, or speech has gravitas and becomes a work of art.

If the Internet has taught us anything, it is that a bad idea remains a bad idea, no matter how many times it gets repeated or how many people have heard it. Media attention alone cannot and should not sanctify anyone. We should never be afraid to judge people, concepts, or art based on merit, not on prevalence and popularity.

• • •

- 119 -
Leaders never fall alone. They take others down with them.

To maintain their tight and coordinated formations, only the lead pilot on teams like the Air Force Thunderbirds or Navy Blue Angels watches his position relative to the ground. Essentially, the lead pilot executes the maneuver. The other pilots are trained to watch the tail or wingtip of the plane next to them, which can be only inches away, to maintain their position and distance. During a Thunderbird practice session 1982, the lead pilot was diving out of a loop maneuver into the desert floor and was supposed to pull level at only one hundred feet over the desert floor. For whatever reason, he failed to pull out in time. The other three pilots, flying in a tight diamond formation with their eyes fixed on his tail or wingtip, followed him with their ordinary precision. Right into the ground. The entire team was killed.

A leader is someone with followers. When the leader fails, the followers either follow or turn aside. But even if the followers pull back or pull out, many are damaged. Political leaders that fail break nations. Financial leaders that fail break lives. Failed business leaders cause hardship. Spiritual leaders that fail break other people's souls. Family leaders that fail break hearts, with bitterness and barrenness as their legacy.

The wise, good, and free person is not a cynic who distrusts all leaders and follows no one. But we should follow wisdom, goodness, and freedom, not people. We should follow and assist leaders that demonstrate, defend, and develop those qualities in and around us. Honor these virtues and learn from them, but be careful about investing too much faith in the humanity of these leaders.

Leaders ought to be sobered by the awareness—like a surgeon or an airline pilot—that they hold lives in their hands. They should be confident enough to do their job and reassure their followers, but every leader should have a healthy fear of failure. And like a surgeon or pilot, they should be rigorous in their preparation and self-evaluation.

• • •

- 120 -

Tolstoy said that happy families are all alike, but that every unhappy family is unhappy in its own way. He was wrong. There are a lot of ways to be happy, but misery and ruined lives follow predictable and well-worn paths.

The Russian writer Leo Tolstoy had wit and a way with words. He was a quotation machine. But while it is catchy, this famous opening line from his 1875 novel *Anna Karenina* is wrong. It operates on the premise that wisdom, goodness, and freedom are simple, while foolishness, evil, and enslavement are complicated and multifaceted. I think he had it backwards.

Goodness and freedom are rich and diverse. There are many ways to be wise, good and free. The wiser you become, the more you realize how much you don't know. A life is not enough time to discover and experience the depths of joy.

Foolish thinking is shallow and dull witted. It has no real knowledge. It cannot create, only pervert and vandalize. "Evil genius" is an oxymoron. The urges of the wicked are boring and predictable. Enslaved to bad impulses that become bad habits, the fate of the fool is a slow motion train wreck.

There are probably no more than a dozen sad and dull ways that families are ruined: adultery, anger, addiction, and abuse; laziness and a lack of love; indebtedness and ingratitude. There are a few others, but this short list has a familiar tragic arc, and leads to unhappy consequences that look eerily familiar.

If you are running down these tracks, get off. Now. It's not a surprise where you'll end up. Choose wisdom, goodness, and freedom.

• • •

- 121 -

Most of us are incompetent at 20% of what we do, and excel at 20% of what we do, and are just average at the other 60%. Spend as much of your time as possible on the 20% you do well.

The wise person knows his limitations, the good person wants to give his best, and the free person doesn't chain himself to things he will never be good at. Of course we all have responsibilities that we cannot walk away from. But as much as possible, collaborate with others to invest yourself where you can be most effective. That takes self-awareness, humility, and the ability to negotiate and exchange value for value. It might also mean letting go of things that you want to be good at, but never will. But how much happier and more free would you be if you could release the burden of your shortcomings to others?

• • •

Are you a leader? Then you have an account of trust and gratitude with your followers. Manage it well. When that account balance reaches zero, you will be an ex-leader.

Think of every leader as having a pile of chips, like casino chips, which represent the trust and gratitude of the followers. Every action the leader takes either earns or loses chips. If the leader does a favor for a follower, he gets a chip. If the leader does something that makes all the followers happier, richer, or safer, they give him hundreds of chips. Conversely, if the leader alienates a follower or the follower's family, he loses five chips. If they leader makes a mistake that hurts a lot of followers, he loses a thousand chips.

When the chips are gone, so is the leader. The only way for him or her to survive is by force, and that subtracts a million chips. When the revolution comes, those leaders retire into exile or at the end of a rope.

If you are a leader, count your chips carefully.

• • •

- 123 -

When the flood is rising, stack sandbags. There is a limit to introspection. Wise and useful people who remain free know when to stop fiddling with their innards and get to work.

The Russian writer Leo Tolstoy famously said that while everyone talks about changing the world, no one talks about changing himself or herself.

Tolstoy had some great quotes. But is this one true?

On the one hand, it absolutely is. If we want to change the world we have to begin with ourselves, for several reasons. First, integrity demands that we not require anything of anyone that we will not do ourselves. If we want a more generous world, then we at least ought to be generous ourselves. Second, we have no control over other people's hearts and actions. We do control our own. And so, spending our effort to change what is beyond our control is pointless. What we can do is become a model for others, and hope that our example influences them. Third, it's foolish to build something that our own actions keep undermining.

On the other hand, there is no shortage of introspection in this world. Every great religion and philosophy has stressed self-improvement. All of that is valuable, but not of unlimited value.

There is a time to contemplate and cultivate inner virtues, and then there is a time to get to work. There is a time to reflect on feelings and fears, and time to shove them aside, put the women and children in the lifeboats, and one's manly duty by going down with the ship. The wise, good, and free person knows the difference.

• • •

- 124 -

Since ancient times, some young people have aspired to be moody and cynical in the mistaken belief that this demonstrates creativity and independent thinking. If this is you, knock it off. It proves nothing except that you're moody and cynical.

The hormonal passions of youth have combined with the myth of the great artist to lead generations of young people astray. It is based on two variations of a logical fallacy:

Many great artists have been moody and cynical.
I am moody and cynical.
I must be a great artist.

Or:

Many great artists have been moody and cynical.
I want to be a great artist.
I must become moody and cynical.

If you are compiling a list of qualities that great artists have had in common, please leave moody and cynical near the bottom. At the top, put things like creative, talented, hard-working, and devoted to one's craft.

Yes, Vincent Van Gogh was tortured by his love for a prostitute and cut off his ear. That is not what made Van Gogh great. He was great in spite of that. If not for that, he might have become even greater.

If you are already talented, cultivate your craft and work hard. Be wise, good, and free and you can unleash your talent. Don't be a fool, with a wicked life, enslaved to bad habits and debt that don't allow you to use your gifts. Knock off the attitude and produce something. Otherwise, you're just a poser.

• • •

- 125 -

My faith teaches me to forgive you, not necessarily to trust you.

There is a tremendous difference between being graceful and gullible. Grace is giving others what they need, not what they deserve. That means forgiving, loving, and sharing. Sometimes, it even means trusting when someone hasn't earned our trust, or has abused it in the past.

But while a graceful person will sometimes award trust as a loving gift, a gullible person trusts out of foolishness, because they are attracted to evil, or because they are enslaved by obligations.

The wise, good, and free person trusts either carefully or graciously, never foolishly.

• • •

- 126 -

You're now self-employed? Congratulations! The good news is that you're now your own boss. The bad news? You're your own boss.

Self-employment sounds like freedom to people who have never experienced it. They imagine working creatively, without constraints. What they do not know is that self-employment can be more constricting that working for someone else. The harsh truth is that it is not a sure path to wisdom, goodness, and freedom.

Self-employment is personal responsibility incarnated. No one restricts you, but no one rescues you, either. You get to discover just how shrewd you are, and how well you can perform. Talent is nothing but potential, results are the only things that count.

Self-employment is a constant test of your ability to perform under pressure in a constantly changing environment. It's a giant obstacle course, a game show that doesn't just reward winners, but punishes losers. The cost of failure is not freedom, but enslavement to debt and even worse consequences.

You provide your own resources; you check your own decisions. You write your own review, which means you have no one to criticize you unfairly, but you also have no one to tell you when you are doing a terrible job. You find that out from your customers. You get to write your own paycheck, but if you don't perform you get nothing.

Self-employment isn't a path to wisdom, goodness, and freedom; it is a lifestyle that rewards the wise, good, and free and harshly penalizes those who are not. Before you jump in, develop those qualities. Jumping into the deep end of the pool is not a winning strategy for learning to swim.

• • •

- 127 -

If you're in some sort of trouble right now, stop thrashing around. Like being stuck in a net or quicksand, the more you struggle, the worse you'll get stuck. Calm down, compose and center yourself, and then methodically work to get free. Don't stop until you're out.

• • •

- 129 -

There is nothing as self-centered as a newborn baby. The purpose of parenting and education is to turn selfish children into adults who can control their impulses and put the needs of others ahead of their own.

We love the idea that children are innocent and good. Have you ever had children? They may not rob banks, but they steal cookies and toys. They may not commit perjury in a court of law, but they lie like a politician. They may not commit murder, but they pull their sister's hair.

We are born full of selfish impulses, which makes sense. A human baby can't help others, it has to protect its own interests and watch out for its own needs. A baby can't tell us what's it's feeling, so it cries to get our attention. But it doesn't care that it is 4 a.m. and the parents have to go to work in three hours. Its needs come first.

We have to learn to care about others. That's what growing up means. Raising or educating a child means training a self-centered soul to love and to serve with consideration and self-control. When our families or schools no longer do that, society begins to break down.

• • •

- 128 -

The biggest influence on an organization's culture is the story that people, both inside and outside, believe about it. You can delegate management, but the real leader of an organization is the one who tells its story.

• • •

- 130 -

The truth floats. You can try to sink it like an inconvenient human body, but it will eventually rise to the surface, at the worst moments, to expose your guilt and shame. So don't drown it, deal with it.

Sometimes, terrible things stay hidden. Most of the time, they don't. Somehow, somewhere, sometime, the truth is going to emerge from wherever you buried it. It might not come out directly, but the consequences of your actions will be felt and someone will trace them back and figure it out. If you think that you are smart and lucky enough to get away with anything, it's proof that you aren't.

You can bury it deeper. That's not wise or good, and won't preserve your freedom. You will drag that secret through your life, always worried that it will be discovered.

You could bring the truth into the light and deal with the consequences. That would be wise and good, and while you may suffer a bit, the truth will set you free.

Or—and this is your wisest, best, and most liberating option—never do anything that you are so ashamed of that you have to bury it in the first place.

• • •

Ten Things I Wish Someone Had Told Me When...

Ten Things I Wish Someone Had Told Me When I Was a Teenager

1. Life speeds up from here, and the stakes just keep getting higher.

I know that you think your life is busy now. Maybe it is, with school, sports, a part-time job, family, and a social life. But after high school, responsibilities will get bigger and come at you faster, like cars and trucks approaching on the highway. And just like standing in the highway, life is lethal—some of your responsibilities will be life-or-death matters. Your perception of time speeds up as your brain processes all these new experiences, and one day you'll wake up and be twenty, thirty, forty…until you're old like me. Don't be afraid of life, but enjoy these years because they are a gift, the pre-season games that let you learn and prepare for what's ahead.

2. Your emotions are not calibrated to reality.

Right now, you can't trust your feelings, especially their volume or intensity. It's like driving a car with untrustworthy gauges: the speedometer may say 60 mph, but it could be 45 or even 72.

See, it's not just that your gauges are off, but they're off by unpredictable amounts, sometimes too high, sometimes too low, sometimes just right. I want to say that the problem fixes itself over time, but the sad truth is that some people never get around to calibrating their emotions to reality. Some drama queens never grow up. It takes experience and effort to adjust your feelings to the real world and to figure out when and how to trust them. For now, rely on the advice and counsel of those who are older and have gone through all of this, whether they're parents, relatives, pastors, teachers, relatives, whomever. Do not ask a friend whose emotional gauges are no more reliable than yours. When you're emotionally worked up, slow down, take some deep breaths, and let someone who is wise, good, and free talk some sense into you.

3. High school is not the high point of your life.

Someday, if you look back on high school as the highlight of your life, then you will have somehow missed the best parts of life. Despite all the heart-wrenching emotions poured out when you sign your friends' yearbooks, most of them will not be your best friends for life. Your boyfriend or girlfriend is almost certainly not your soul mate, so *do not* trust them with your soul! You will probably never go back and visit your high school (why?), and if you are still proudly displaying your high school memorabilia or talking about your high school accomplishments twenty years from now, then you lost twenty years somewhere along the way. I'm not saying that high school is bad, or that you should hate it or not treasure it. But it's a brief passage along the way to things that are bigger and far more meaningful than you can understand right now.

4. At this point in your life you can't achieve great success, but you can fail spectacularly.

As a teenager, you can't achieve too much, unless you become a teenage movie star or get drafted directly into the NBA. But while even those rare kids might get famous and make a lot of money, too many learn about just how badly you can fail at this age. And when I say fail, I mean the belly flop into a pit of acid and have your remains mauled by a cougar type of failure. In fact, if dumb enough, that exact scenario could actually happen (it probably has, somewhere). And while successes come and go, some failures are forever: teens who become paraplegics for life because they drove drunk or distracted; teens who got pregnant because of loose morals loosened further by alcohol; teens who got criminal records or a drug addiction or an embarrassing tattoo; teens who ruined their education or family forever because they were careless or emotionally immature or downright dumb.

You're walking through a minefield. Watch where you put your foot.

5. The adults around you understand a lot more than you think they do.

I know what you're thinking: *they're so old, and they never felt what I feel, or had a [fill in the blank] like I do.* But you're going to just have to trust me on this one: they were your age, felt exactly what you're feeling, and did exactly what you're doing (or are thinking about doing). They hated their parents (your grandparents) sometimes. They had boyfriends and girlfriends (probably not your mom or dad), and everything that comes with that—even that dumb notion you have that no one could ever understand how special your love is. If they don't support whatever it is you want to do it's not because they don't understand, it's because they *do,* and they want you to learn from their mistakes. If they've been where you are, why wouldn't you want them to lead you through? Please tell them what's going on, and really listen to what they have to say.

6. You are not special.

I know, mom and dad say you are, but come on: they're your mom and dad. You are special, *to them.* I know that you feel alone a lot, but you aren't alone in what you're feeling. This is your first time around the block, and everything looks so unique and strange and intense. It seems that way to everyone the first time. This is just you discovering yourself and the world. You are not the smartest person in the world nor the dumbest. I know that you have ideas in your head that seem so original, but they aren't. I know you think that no one else in the whole world can possibly understand what you're going through, but that's pretty much what every teenager has thought since Adam and Eve had Cain and Abel. Like I said earlier, your emotions are not calibrated to reality yet. So, no: you do not have superpowers, and you will probably not be one of the ten most significant figures in history. On the other hand, if you feel isolated and worthless and depressed, please find a wise, good, and free adult whose been around the block a few times who will tell you that you are OK and that everything is going to work out. Because it will, as long as you recognize that this is just life, and you can grow up into it so that it fits.

7. You don't always pick good friends.

You're already sick of your parents telling you they don't trust this or that friend or that they don't like your boyfriend or girlfriend. "How can you say that?!" you demand. "You don't even know them!" OK, maybe not. Of course, it's possible that you don't know them, either. See, at your age, you don't have a lot of experience reading and filtering people, and you can't put clues about people into context. You will learn, eventually, but mostly by getting burned or having your heart broken. Most of the mistakes you can make right now come from making bad decisions about people. If some of the wise, good, and free older people around you see some red flags in your friends, pay attention.

8. Give your family a break.

Yes, they drive you crazy, they are unfair, you fight with them, and they don't let you have any fun. Yada, yada, yada. Please give them a break. They are your family, the only one you will ever have. These years, when you are still living with them, will be over before you know it: we grow up, we move out, and we move on. There will be new seasons in your relationship with your family, and those are great, too. But don't be in too much of a hurry to move on. You will look back on these few quick years for the rest of your life. And unless you have a seriously messed up family (which do exist, but see the next point), let me tell you a secret: they love you more than you can or will ever understand. They work as hard as they can to provide as good a life for you as they can. Yes, they make a thousand mistakes, but they are mistakes: they wouldn't do anything to intentionally harm you. Despite all their flaws, they are doing their best for you. Please give them a break, and do your best for them.

9. Knock off the whole anger and victimhood routine.

I suspect that if someone took the effort to give you this book and have you read this passage (because I know you didn't go buy the book yourself and read this many pages in), then you are not a real victim. In fact, if someone gave you this to read, my guess is that they are trying to send you a hint and buy you a clue: please drop the whiny, rebellious attitude. Some teens really do have legitimate complaints. They are victims of abuse, neglect, genuine hardship, or great injustice. Are you sure that you are one of them? If not, then you're acting like this because you are self-centered and unappreciative of all the gifts and advantages you've been given in life. That attitude will corrupt your soul, lead you to make stupid and dangerous choices, drive those who love you away, and poison your opportunities. Stop it.

10. Happiness is a choice.

Happiness is not something that happens to you which you cannot control, like the flu. It's something that you can choose, and you need to learn how make that choice early in life because you're going to have to make that choice almost every single day from here on out. There is so much you will not have control over: the economy, your health, the health of your loved ones, the actions of other people, tsunamis. If happiness is just a condition that happens to you when things are going well, you are going to spend a lot of your life unhappy. So right now, begin learning to find joy and contentment in any circumstances, under any conditions. Learn the secret of choosing to be cheerful, controlling stress, and cultivating a happy heart. That doesn't mean you have to settle in life for less than you dream, but it does mean that when your dreams are delayed you are not devastated. You will be able to weather life's storms and come out the other side intact.

Ten Things I Wish Someone Had Told Me When I Got Married

1. Choose your habits carefully.

We are creatures of habit and routine, and that tendency is one of the things that make marriage work. It's exhausting to even imagine waking up every day to a partner with random behaviors. We count on our husband or wife liking the same foods, keeping the same schedule, and reacting in predictable ways. Over the years, we fall into these grooves that are very difficult to get out of, and our spouses digs their own grooves parallel to ours, which is why we should choose those grooves very carefully. Bad habits developed early in the marriage—in the bedroom, in the checkbook, around the dinner table, with the in-laws or children, or during arguments—become very difficult to change over the years. They doom us to the same conflicts over and over (see Item #3 below) or cause long term hurts that remain open abrasions and never heal. In some cases they are fatal to the marriage. Within the first few years, you set habits for the next fifty. Choose carefully.

2. Money matters.

I know it shouldn't, but it does, although not necessarily in the same way that some people think it does. It is true that money cannot buy happiness, and you can certainly be happy without a lot of money. But a marriage is a lot of things, and most of them involve money. You are a household, a home, a family unit—all of these involve spending money for shelter, food, clothing, etc. And so, money will flow through your marriage almost daily. Sometimes, it will be on the surface, and sometimes, it will be like a subterranean river or aquifer, but almost everything you do together will require money, or decisions about money, or the handling of money. Again, more money doesn't mean a better marriage. But the quality of your marriage absolutely will be affected by how you think about it, how you make decisions about it, and how you handle it. If you do those things together and well, then you can barely have two sticks to rub together and you can live in marital bliss, and more won't necessarily make you happier. If you are incompatible in the area of money and resources, you could have a mountain of it and be miserable together—lots of rich people are. Your future together depends not so much on your financial worth as your financial compatibility.

3. You will have the same half-dozen fights for the rest of your life.

You won't have six hundred fights in your marriage; you'll have six fights a hundred times. The things that lead to real conflict in marriage are our basic points of incompatibility. And unless you married a complete stranger, there are only a handful of those. But here's the problem: most of us don't change that much over time. We want to, we try to, but it's very difficult. And so, to mix a metaphor, wherever our sharp edges clash, our gears grind again and again. Couple A has never fought about issue X, but Couple B has snipped at each other about it for thirty years. Couple A gets so tired of issue Y that they get a divorce over it, but it has never occurred to Couple B to even disagree over it. The solution is obvious, but very difficult: isolate and contain these half dozen problems like the Centers for Disease Control quarantining a virus outbreak, and then try to destroy them with every resource you've got. It probably means that both of you will have to change your shape a little bit at those conflict points so that they don't grind as badly. Every now and then there will be a flare-up on those border points. But when they come, celebrate and enjoy the ninety-four points of agreement between you while you learn to live with the six perpetual challenges.

4. You can't be sure about the the future but you can be sure about your behavior.

There are no guarantees of what will happen during a marriage, but the whole point of a marriage is to guarantee how we will react, whatever happens. We promise to make it work through good times and bad, sickness and health, wealth and poverty, until death do us part. Whatever life throws at us, we can still choose how we will react, what we will do, and who we will be. But what about the spouse who breaks their vows? A faithful spouse can still wind up with a broken marriage. But they can decide that they will not be the one to break it.

When we allow the possibility, no matter how slender, that we can break our vows if things aren't turning out like we expected, then failure has become an option and a day will come when that becomes like a light that brings hope in a dark place. If we can break our vows, we will be sorely tempted to do it. Decide that, as much as it is up to you, failure is not an option for your marriage, and that whatever else happens, you will be a promise keeper.

5. It's not about you or even the two of you. Your marriage affects more people than you will ever know.

You can have a private sexual relationship if that's what you want. But marriage is not a private affair, and it never has been. That's why we have witnesses, sign legal documents, and record marriages in public records. A marriage binds two people, but it also joins extended families, entwines property, becomes part of the fabric of communities and churches, makes friends, and produces children. Why do you think those two hundred people were at your wedding? To celebrate that you were having, or going to have, sex and play house with someone? Your marriage is a unit, the basic unit, of society, and society is invested in it. When it fails, lots of people are affected. When lots of marriages fail, it costs society dearly. You are responsible, and expected, to hold your place in the line in the world's defense against chaos. Do not abandon your post, because others will suffer if you do.

6. Take care of yourself so you have something good to give to your spouse.

In marriage you give yourself as a gift to another person. But if you let yourself deteriorate, what do you have to offer? Is your personality enjoyable? Are your habits responsible and considerate? Is your heart hopeful, helpful, and honorable? Are your finances in order? And, yes: is your body as attractive as you can reasonably make it? Don't be surprised if your spouse's enthusiasm for you sags when your flabby soul or body is sagging because of neglect and self-abuse. Take responsibility for maintaining and even improving yourself. Coldness at the dinner table or in the bedroom is not all his or her fault. Do your best, and offer your best. If he or she doesn't, encourage, but don't nag. Nagging gets you no where. Set an example for giving the best of yourself to the one you love.

7. Here is the biggest reason marriages fail: two people set out for different destinations.

Imagine two sailboats, setting out from the harbor in San Diego, California at the same time, headed to Tahiti. At first, they sail alongside each other. But over time, they gradually drift apart because they have punched different coordinates into their navigation computers. The differences weren't great enough to notice before departure—the two skippers would have caught the error if they were headed for different continents—but they were off by a degree of latitude. Over a couple of thousand miles of open ocean, that one degree difference means hundreds of miles, and eventually they lose each other over the horizon.

You can never check your navigation too much. Before the marriage, while getting married, every month or week or even day during the marriage, keep comparing and recalibrating. Ask if you are going in the same direction. If not, you will have to make adjustments, or you will lose each other over the horizon. Who makes the adjustment? Who's right, and who's wrong? Most of the time, both of you need to make a course correction. Especially because our destinations change over time as we grow and learn and encounter the surprises of life. Get help and work it out.

8. Sex matters.

Really, sex is the reason we get married in the first place. We could have all sorts of other relationships to meet our needs: friends, business partners, roommates, etc. But a man and a woman get married because they are a man and a woman, and they come together as one flesh, most of the time to produce children. Really, that's the whole point.

There is more to marriage than sex—a lot more—but there should never be less. In other words, if we take sex out, all we are is roommates, parents, business partners, sometimes friends. To put sex in the terminology of formal logic (something we are not normally inclined to do), it is not a sufficient condition for a happy marriage, but it is a necessary one. When we can no longer be intimate, to merge our flesh and not know where one of us begins and the other ends, we have ceased to be man and wife.

But, but, but...yes, there are medical conditions, separations for work or war, seasons when children render us too exhausted to do it. Obviously, all that is true. But those are burdens to be borne with joy or obstacles to be overcome with determination. My wife and I have a friend who says if you can eat outside, you should. In the same spirit, if we can make love, we should. It's what makes us married.

9. Neither of you is the model for what the other has to become.

You're not supposed to become like her, or she like you. Together, the two of you are becoming a third, new thing.

The Bible says that a man shall leave his mother and father and cleave to his wife and they shall become one flesh. We are both supposed to grow up, blending aspects of each other's identity into our own and adding into the mix qualities that neither of us had as we learn about life together.

Of course, this isn't easy. We aren't destined to become like our parents, but that's the gravity well into which we are constantly being pulled. It takes energy to escape it. And our own selfish nature constantly demands that our spouse take on our values and style.

It's one of the greatest joys of life to grow into another person as you both grow older together like two small saplings whose roots and branches entwine over the decades so that you can no longer tell where one ends and the other begins.

10. Never criticize your spouse to others. That cracks the door to other disloyalties.

It is so tempting to vent our frustration with our spouse to a friend. We rationalize that a good friend will understand, offering comfort and advice. And when we can't find a good friend, we're tempted to criticize our spouse behind their back to an acquaintance, or even a stranger. But when we do, we create a confidant and forge an emotional alliance against the one person in the world to whom we owe complete loyalty. It feels innocent, at first. But in small and subtle ways, we are driving a wedge in our marriage. Our wife or husband becomes "her" or "him," the Other whom we seek support against. That support may be nothing more than a nod of the head, a chuckle, or a pat on the arm. But an important shift has occurred. And what begins with that small gesture doesn't always end there. Do not open the door to disloyalty to your husband or wife, even a little bit.

Ten Things I Wish Someone Had Told Me When I Started a Business

1. It will be harder than you think it will be, in different ways than you expect.

I know that you know it will be hard to own a business. Not many people are foolish enough to think it will be easy. But you don't realize just how demanding it will be. The reason is that your business is a projection of yourself. All of your great qualities are what's compelling you to start it. Those are the assets, or products. But there are other parts of you that aren't so helpful. If you haven't learned what those are yet, you're about to find out. Those aspects of your personality or dimensions of your life are going to be your business's liabilities and its weak points. Your business will be more challenging than you expected because you will be mostly fighting against yourself.

Add into that mix all sorts of external challenges. Every year, the government in America makes it more difficult to succeed as a business owner. You would think that the community wants you to succeed, and in a way they do, because then you are an asset to be taxed. You will be expected to share your success with those who haven't even tried, and to give your "fair share" to those who contribute nothing.

There will be fierce competition, customers who pay late or not at all, and employees who don't care about the business as much as you do. In the end, running a business will take all of your creativity and intelligence, energy and endurance, discipline, and confidence. You must remain hopeful, patient, and self-controlled. To succeed while remaining wise, good, and free will test your character as much as anything you try to do in life.

2. You are a boss, not a buddy.

If you have an empathetic, or even sympathetic personality, then you want to bond with your workers. For a variety of reasons, you may need to be liked and even loved by the people that you work with. And you may be lonely as a leader. All of that will make what I'm about to say harder for you to accept, but here it is: you cannot be a friend to your employees. You can be friendly, but as soon as you hire and pay someone who works at your pleasure, your relationship with them ceases to be a level playing field.

I'm not saying that you are better than them or that you have to be domineering. But it really isn't fair to them to pretend that you are their friend. Because they know that the relationship really isn't equal, since you sign their paycheck. If you try to be their buddy, it puts them in an awkward position. They can't tell you what they really think, or share their real struggles or concerns with you, because that involves sharing things which might jeopardize their employment. They might love you and be loyal to you, but they cannot genuinely share their world with you because your money supports their family. They can't risk vulnerability, and that is an essential quality of friendship. Nor is it fair to you for them to assume your friendship, either. You may need to make difficult decisions which affect their livelihood. And you may need to give some directive that they don't like. Familiarity and friendship might make their obedience, or your ability to demand it, complicated.

It *is* lonely at the top. If you can't tell people no, get out now.

3. If you want to work for a non-profit, then go do that.

I meet a lot of people who want to start businesses so that they can have the resources to contribute to some charitable cause. I think that is wonderful, admirable, and responsible. I hope that so many people buy this book that I will have extra resources to contribute to causes that I believe in.

But beneath that, I'm deeply concerned for a lot of these people because I fear they are setting their business up for failure. Your business model cannot be a means to an end, or it will never work. No, the goal in life is not to get as rich as we can be. But a business that sees its core activity as overhead to its real purpose, is working against itself.

Whether you build cars, design flower gardens, or sell lemonade from a stand in front of your parent's house, 99% of owning a business is selling something for more money than it costs to make it. It really is that simple. If that's not for you, don't start a business.

I know you want to be socially responsible and change the world; so do I. But you also have to be honest with yourself and others. If you don't really want to run a business, then don't. But don't waste your time, money, and opportunities (and other peoples' as well) on something that your heart isn't in. You won't be doing yourself, your employees, or your customers any good by pretending to care about what you are doing. If you really want to work for a non-profit, then go do that.

4. This will be your life.

Don't start a business if you're looking for a job without a boss. That's one of the biggest and most tragic mistakes that new business owners can make. It's easy to do when you're working for someone else. You get frustrated at taking orders and having limited resources. You want to control your own destiny, to be captain of your own ship, and have the freedom to explore the sea of life without restraint.

But your own business never gives you the freedom that you think it will. Sure, you are in charge and get to make the decisions. But all those decisions have consequences attached to them. Your choices affect not only yourself, but your employees and their families. Your life savings and all your assets are tied up in the business, and you can't walk away when you get sick of it. It takes far more time than you ever expected. You are never off the job, because you are always responsible. Your family's fate and time gets wrapped up in the business, and the separation between work and home, between professional and personal, blurs.

Starting a business is not taking a better job, it's taking on a different kind of life. It has the potential for enormous rewards, but it comes with great costs. Choose carefully, because once you jump into this pool, it's very difficult to climb back out.

5. If you don't like thinking about and dealing with money, turn around now.

What's the role of money in your business? Every day you will have to figure out how to make more of it than you spend. And you cannot be emotional about money, or you will not be able to handle it. That's all I have to say about that. If that's not you, don't do this.

6. There are a thousand ways to screw up everyday.

Every day in business is a new opportunity for compromise or stupidity. Every day you will be tempted to cut corners, produce garbage, or abandon your principles.

Every day you will come dangerously close to making poor decisions out of laziness, stress, or ignorance. Every day you will come close to losing a deal, a customer, or a good employee. You will fall in love with bad ideas and let good ideas slip away because you're too tired or don't have time to consider them. And all of these screw ups will cost you. Enough of them and it will cost you everything.

What's the solution? Keep your head on a swivel. Stay sharp and frosty. Get a good night's sleep, don't send an email that you haven't thought through, don't speak out of anger, don't get lazy about the details, keep a sharp eye on the money, set a good example for your team, be a lifelong learner, be an innovator but rely on what you know works.

There are a thousand mistakes you can make, and sometimes it feels like you are just trying to avoid them rather than creating success. But if ninety percent of success is just showing up, then ninety-five percent is showing up and not screwing up when you get there.

7. Be very careful who your partners are.

Just as young people can screw up their life by picking the wrong friends, you can doom your business (and maybe your career and credit) by picking the wrong partner.

When you start dreaming up a business idea with other people, it's a lot like dating. Everyone is optimistic, imaginative, witty, and on their best behavior. Like dating, you may even go to fun places to plan the business. You sit in a favorite bar or coffee shop, daydreaming and drawing on a napkin while forming your own little inside jokes. It's you against the world, and you get a warm feeling of belonging from your own little, brand new culture. Sure, there are some areas of disagreement, but you convince yourself that those will work themselves out over time.

But like in a badly chosen marriage, the little tips above the waves during the dates can turn out to be giant icebergs under the water when you move in together. You might soon discover how your partner handles money, their people skills, their work habits, their personal habits, their work hours and ethic, and a thousand other points of incompatibility. And like a bad marriage, there is no easy way out of a bad business partnership. Money, assets, customers, employees, and reputations are all at stake. So choose your partners wisely. Don't take on any partners that you don't absolutely need.

8. Don't carry underperforming people or products.

If you carry an underperforming employee out of compassion, that's admirable. But ask yourself whether it's compassion or a fear of conflict and change. If you are trying to sell a product or service and not enough people are buying it, why are you sticking with it? Is it a fear of change? Inability to give up on a dream? Lack of creativity, or energy? How long will you ride a dying horse?

Can you help the underperforming employee to succeed? If you can, you should. Can you improve your product or service so it is competitive? If you can, it's easier than inventing and introducing something new. But if you can't make someone or something better, then you are doing no one any good by denying reality and delaying change that could be good for everyone concerned.

Loyalty is a wonderful thing, a true virtue. So is persistence. But if someone or something is not producing or performing for your business, fix or drop them or it before you go bankrupt.

9. You are the problem.

As I said in the first item on this list, your business is a projection of yourself. All your great qualities are the assets or products. But the parts of you that aren't so helpful are your business's liabilities and weak points. If your company is struggling, it may very well be because you are its own worst enemy. Every day, you fight against the dark side of your own nature, whatever that is, manifested in your business. For one owner, it might be his laziness and carelessness about details that influence a sloppy culture among the employees. In another company, the owner's poor people skills might create a chaotic and conflict-ridden company with lousy customer service. Whatever the raw sewage is running through a company, it usually flows down from the top. An organization cannot be better than the people who lead it. If a leader's character is weaker than that of the people he leads, either he or they will go. You want to fix your company? Physician, heal thyself.

10. Know where every penny is, at every second.

Worthwhile pilots or sea captains know their machines intimately. They know every weld, every system, every rattle and hum coming from the engines. They know every instrument and what those instruments are telling them. They can feel the vital essences—fuel, oil, hydraulic fluid, electricity—flowing through the veins of their aircraft or ship. When something is amiss, they can react because they can instantly imagine in their mind what the problem is and what their options are.

Any business owner worth his or her salt knows where every penny in the business is and how it got there. Money is the blood of business, its life force, and the point of its existence. A business owner that doesn't pay attention to the money, who can't read the balance sheet or the cash flow report, cannot command the organization or react to problems when they arise. They quickly become ex-business owners.

Ten Myths That are Ruining Your Results and Crippling Your Career

There is no shortage of talks and books about successful thinking.

But too much of what currently passes for success thinking doesn't doesn't actually lead to success. Far too often, it is designed to make the thinker feel successful, not to increase performance or produce great products.

In fact, many of these "successful" thought patterns are actually counterproductive and work against performance. Each is a seductive myth of the "new economy," which works against the only economy that really matters: the reality of the marketplace.

1. The Paralysis of Potential

Popular "success thinking" encourages individuals to be comforted by their potential and for businesses to invest in the possible rather than the probable. Success gurus justify this speculation with a few carefully chosen anecdotes of inventors or discoverers who came up with something radically new. But in most cases, these anecdotes leave out the fact that these discoverers largely made incremental progress by focusing on the achievable. In the "new economy," fascination with the possible is distracting us from the probable and keeping us from producing what is practical.

2. The Peril of Passion

Popular thinking tells us that having "passion for our work" is key to success. In truth, passion is only useful as a predictor of performance. No one pays anyone to be passionate about their work. In in the marketplace, it is the quality of the product that matters. Passion may make your work more enjoyable, but it doesn't make it more valuable to others. In fact, passion for our work may actually be counterproductive, as it makes us unable to see our product as others see it and leaves us puzzled as to why they aren't as enthusiastic as we are.

3. The Promise of Pay

We all want to earn as much as we can for our work. But focusing on the amount of money we aspire to earn tomorrow can cause us to deceive ourselves about how much we are worth today. It is easy to fall into the trap of believing that if we were paid more, we would do a better job and that the only thing holding us back from doing our best is the pay and perks that the top people in our field get. The truth is that more money will keep us doing what we are doing and perhaps make it easier to focus on doing it. Money only rewards great performance, it doesn't produce it.

4. The Puzzle of Personality

Contemporary psychology has given us wonderful insights into the complexity of personality in the workplace. Understanding our personalities can help us work better and smarter. But dwelling on our personality traits and those of our coworkers distracts us from focusing on our products. Great things and great services come from people with a wide range of personality types. The marketplace cares less about who you are than what you do.

5. The Prevarication of Politics

"Prevarication" means the telling or spreading of a falsehood, and too often we lie to ourselves about why we lost a debate, or a deal, or even a job. When things don't go our way, we are tempted to blame it on "politics" in the organization. It is easier to believe that a political agenda was the cause of our setback than to accept that there might have been a substantive issue, because that would mean that we might have been wrong. It is always easier to attribute bad or shallow motives to our opponents than to consider them rational people who might come to different conclusions about an issue, a product, or us.

6. The Pretension of Profession

Professionalism is important, but it can also be self-serving. Sometimes, we like to pretend that our degree, title, or experience uniquely qualifies us to do something that really isn't all that unique. We sniff and sneer and get defensive when an outsider produces something that's as good as anything we could have done. There are good reasons why some industries should insist on professional standards and good reasons why consumers should hire qualified professionals. But if we are not careful, it can become mere guild or union protectionism. If the only thing standing between ourselves and our competition is our defensive demand that consumers buy from us because of our professional status, then it won't be long before our "unprofessional" competition gets the consumer to compare our products. If that happens, we are setting ourselves up for a hard fall.

7. The Paradox of Perfection

The paradox of perfection is illustrated by the story of a a mathematician and an engineer, who find themselves magically transported to a vast hall with a beautiful woman at one end. An ethereal voice tells them that at the top of each hour, with the ringing of the clock's bells, they may advance half the distance to the woman.

The mathematician immediately throws up his hands in disgust. "Well, what's the point? At that rate, I'll never get there."

But as the first bell rings, the engineer enthusiastically runs halfway across the hall. "Are you crazy?" shouts the mathematician from the starting point, where he has sat down and given up. "Don't you realize that by halving the distance, you will never get to her?"

"That's OK," shouts back the engineer. "Eventually, I'll get close enough for my purposes!"

Perfection is an abstraction, a mathematical concept unattainable in human endeavors. Perfectionists often quit, because reality can never live up to their standards, and they would rather not try than to try and fail. They are not usually happy people. Winners know that eventually, with hard work, creativity, and patience, they will get close enough for their purposes.

8. The Pivot of the Problem

Question: What's the only problem that matters in a business transaction?

Answer: The problem of the person paying the money. So the problem that counts is the employer's problem, not the employee's, the customer's rather than the seller's.

When the problem is pivoted, performance suffers. If the employee begins to think that the employer exists to solve his problem (i.e. he needs a job) rather than the other way around (the employer has a job that needs to be done), the employer-employee relationship is going to break down. And when the seller begins to think that they buyer exists to solve her problem (i.e. she has a truckload of sombreros to sell—see page 101), then the sale isn't going to happen.

To fix these kinds of breakdowns, the relationship needs to be spun around, pivoted on the problem that really counts, so that all the parties are clear on the purpose of the contract.

9. The Prestige of the Past

You cannot live too long on past accomplishments. You can get away with it for awhile, but eventually, someone is going to ask what you've done lately. When you're self-image is bathed in the prestige of past glory, you are marinating in your own ego, which will leave you soft and vulnerable. There are always hungry competitors innovating and putting new points on the scoreboard. Yes, brand equity is real, but so is running out of goodwill with your employer or customer.

10. The Power of Praise

Encouragement is vital to our well being. It kindles our optimism and carries us through setbacks. It teaches us by positive reinforcement instead of beating us with endless criticism.

But excessive praise insulates us from realistic self-assessment. When we just hear how great we are, we forget that we aren't great. We indulge our weaknesses and ignore our vulnerabilities. We stop improving and innovating.

Don't take the praise you receive too seriously, and don't spend too much time listening to it. Seek out encouragement for your effort and virtue, but be cautious of those who only puff you up without coaching you in how to grow.

Five Ways to Fail in Business, and Six to Succeed

Five Ways to Fail in Business

There are actually dozens, if not thousands, of ways to fail in business. But these five run through the stories of fizzled careers with a sad consistency. They are important landmarks on the map to the minefield of professional failure. We all might make one of these mistakes at some point, and they can be left behind with great effort. But every one of them is corrosive to professional success. If any one of them is your normal mode of operation, knock it off right now and learn to practice its opposite trait on the second list.

1. Cost More Than You Are Worth

Does your product or service take more from people in money, time, energy, trouble, etc. than it gives to them? Do you cost too much to your employees, colleagues, suppliers, government regulators, etc.? As soon as this equation is upside down for you, your days in that business are numbered.

2. Misunderstand Your Marketplace

What do customers need or want? Why do they, or would they, buy from you to meet those needs? Where else can they get their needs and wants met? If you don't know your customer or the constantly shifting dynamics of your marketplace, your days in that business are numbered.

3. Think Like a Entitled Victim

Never believe that customers owe you their business or that you deserve to succeed. People buy to meet their interests, not yours. Never dwell on any unfairness that you think you've suffered. While you feel sorry for yourself and nurse your wounds and grudges, your competition is wooing your customers. Passivity is a prescription for business failure.

4. Lose Your Liberty

Business success requires flexibility, adaptability, creativity, and resiliency. All of those require freedom to think, choose, and act. The more you limit your freedom—through debt, unnecessary overhead costs, bad commitments and contracts, your own bad habits, etc.—the more narrow your room to maneuver in a constantly changing marketplace. Self-imposed limitations shorten your shelf life as a business.

5. Value Information over Knowledge

Know what you know, and what you don't know. Know what you need to know, and what you don't. In every business, there are thousands of bits of data. Information about everything from the environment to your customers, to your competition, and to your resources. Knowledge is information that you are sure of, and that is useful. Focus on what you know. If you need to know something but don't, learn. Other information might be interesting, but if you aren't sure of it and can't use it, it's a distraction. Don't waste your time on useless information, or your days in business will be numbered.

...And Six to Succeed.

None of these six items will guarantee success, which is a complex and multivariable equation. But they run consistently through so many success stories that they might be said to be necessary (but not sufficient) conditions for doing well in the business world. At the very least, practicing these six will guarantee that your career is the best kind.

1. Add Value in Every Transaction

Every time you interact with someone in business, give them more value than you take. Leave them feeling like they got the better end of the deal. Treat everyone this way, not just customers, and your business will have an advantage over the competition.

2. Solve Someone Else's Problem, Not Your Own.

Customers don't buy to meet your needs. They buy out of self-interest, to meet their needs and fill their wants. Understand the demand, and supply it, and you will give people every reason to buy from you.

3. Be Resilient and Optimistic

Business is an obstacle course, across the rolling deck of a ship, while your competition throws stuff at you, and the customer keeps moving the goalposts. Fun, huh? Change is constant. Every minute you spend whining about change and refusing to adapt, you fall further behind. Remain resilient. If you fall down, get up, if you have a bad day, make tomorrow better. And have an optimistic attitude, because it shapes how you behave and how others see you. Adaptability, confidence, and a positive disposition can take you further in business than a brilliant mind or product.

4. Fiercely Favor Freedom

Love your liberty, and don't give any of it away unless you have to. Don't take on debt you don't need. Don't commit to anything that you don't have to or don't want to. Don't burden your business with unnecessary overhead costs. Don't let bad habits make you sluggish and impotent. Preserve enough energy to react, room to maneuver, and time to think and create. Be free to change and grow, and you can.

5. Seek Wisdom

Learn to recognize what is true and what is false, what is useful and what is wasteful, what builds up and what tears down. Know what is good, and how to be and do good. Cultivate sound judgment and the ability to process better decisions faster by disregarding distractions. Being smart has value, but it isn't always a factor in success. Successful business leaders aren't always smart, but they are all shrewd.

6. Success is Being Good and Doing Good

Money isn't the only measure of success, nor its only reward. A business that loses money can't be said to be succeeding, but the one with the biggest bottom line might not be the best or the one that you want to own. If it were, we'd all strive to be investment bankers or run international drug cartels. Be profitable, but earn that profit by being a good person, with a good reputation, who provides a good product, that brings good value to good people. You will succeed enough to be happy, and to enjoy the love and loyalty of your family and friends. What more do you want?

About the Author

Greg Smith is a professional writer and speaker. He works in a variety of genres, across a wide range of topics, and frequently collaborates with other authors. He is the owner and chief creative officer of Black Lake Studio & Press in Holland, Michigan, where he lives with his wife Linda and their two children. To learn more about Greg, please visit:

www.SmithGreg.com

Made in the USA
Charleston, SC
24 April 2012